# The River
# of Light

# BOOKS BY LAWRENCE KUSHNER

*The Book of Letters:*
*A Mystical Hebrew Alef-Bait*
2nd edition
Jewish Lights Publishing

*The Book of Words:*
*Talking Spirirual Life, Living Spiritual Talk*
Jewish Lights Publishing

*Honey from the Rock:*
*Visions of Jewish Mystical Renewal*
Jewish Lights Publishing

*The River of Light:*
*Spirituality, Judaism, Consciousness*
Jewish Lights Publishing

*The Invisible Chariot:*
*An Introduction to Jewish Mysticism*
*for Young Adults*
*(with Deborah Kerdeman)*
Alternatives in Religious Education Press

*The Book of Miracles:*
*Jewish Spirituality for*
*Children to Read to Their Parents*
*and Parents to Read to Their Children*
Union of American Hebrew Congregations Press

*Sparks Beneath the Surface:*
*A Spiritual Commentary on the Torah*
*(with Kerry Olitzky)*
Jason Aronson Publishers

*God Was in This Place & I, i Did Not Know:*
*Finding Self, Spirituality and Ultimate Meaning*
Jewish Lights Publishing

# The River of Light

נהרא דנהורא

*Nahara DiNehora*

## Spirituality, Judaism, Consciousness

## Lawrence Kushner

JEWISH LIGHTS Publishing
Woodstock, Vermont

**The River of Light**
Copyright ©1990 and 1981 by Lawrence Kushner

Biblical quotations throughout the text are in the author's own translation.

Fourth paperback printing, Enhanced Reprint, JEWISH LIGHTS Publishing,
Woodstock, Vermont, 1995
Third paperback printing, Enhanced Reprint, JEWISH LIGHTS Publishing, 1993
Second paperback printing, Enhanced Reprint, JEWISH LIGHTS Publishing, 1990
First hardcover printing, Rossel Books, Chappaqua, NY, 1981
First paperback printing, Harper & Row, Publishers, Inc., NY, 1981

*Library of Congress Cataloging-in-Publication Data*

Kushner, Lawrence , 1943-
The river of light.

1. Judaism—Miscellanea.  2. Mysticism—Judaism—Miscellanea.
I. Title.
BM723.K88      296.3

ISBN  1-879045-03-6:  $14.95 (pb)


10  9  8  7  6  5  4  3

Cover design by Irving Perkins Associates
Cover photograph by Lawrence Kushner

Manufactured in the United States of America


Published by JEWISH LIGHTS Publishing
A Division of LongHill Partners, Inc.
P.O. Box 237
Sunset Farm Offices, Route 4
Woodstock, Vermont 05091
Tel: (802) 457-4000  Fax: (802) 457-4004

*for*
*S. T. H.*

# Contents

# *Foreword*

## to the second printing of
### *The River of Light*

In rabbinic school we used to tease one another about how even great Rabbis only have a few good sermons in them. And that throughout their preaching career, all they accomplish are variations on a few themes. In retrospect, I realize now, with some embarrassment, that *The River of Light* is nothing more than a prolonged commentary on the first three pages—the letter Aleph—of my first book, *The Book of Letters* (Harper & Row, 1975; JEWISH LIGHTS, 1990).

RIVER explores themes initially assembled in *LETTERS* which continue to animate my imagination: barely audible noise, the name of God, the life of the first Jew, the primordial human archetype, the nature of consciousness, the relationship of self to God, and above all, how they are all interrelated to one another. To me, they all seem to be part of the same sermon. In that sense, *The River of Light* remains my most ambitious shot at a "unified field theory" for Jewish theology.

From a literary point of view, I believe *RIVER* is also noteworthy. It may be one of the very few times that a sustained (and systematic) theology was written *within* a Midrash. Of course, the Rabbis of the Talmud constantly taught about God's relationship to human beings, history, and the world through imagining brief sub- and super-texts to the bible. But *The River of Light* does so for an entire book. And in the process it tries to integrate the classic themes of creation, revelation and redemption, with their contemporary counterparts of self-realization, consciousness, and personal transformation. All of these ideas are set within the larger matrix of a spiritual journey made by Abraham, our father.

RIVER is certainly too ambitious for what is only a little book. Indeed, I now realize that it too is only the table of contents of a much larger one which I pray to be able to complete.

LSK
August 1990, Elul 5750
Sandwich, MA

# Introduction

Occasionally, a single word appears at the confluence of great intellectual currents. A word that seems to belong in each, yet combine all. In this generation, "consciousness" is such a word. Possessed of almost poetic promise, it is also the legitimate object of scientific inquiry. It brings together many of the strands of psychotherapy, from Freud to transpersonal psychology. It appears on the outer edges of theoretical physics and biochemistry. It is at home both in theology and mythology. Perhaps, we imagine, it is the location of a long-awaited synthesis of some of the great truth traditions of humanity. I have tried to bring together these several readings of consciousness in the spiritual idiom of the Hebrew Bible and subsequent rabbinic tradition. They are arranged according to a journey Abraham, our father, once made; a journey that lead him beyond the scriptural text of his daily life, all the way back to the primordial light of consciousness itself.

The following chapters chronicle that legend and attempt to describe what might happen to someone who ventures on such a journey: a journey that is nothing less than the evolution of consciousness. And because human consciousness—and probably all

of creation—comes from the yearning of the Holy One of Being
to attain self-awareness, it is a story about God. The story of our
role in the coming into being of the One of Being. So it is also a
theology of consciousness, or, if you will permit, ongoing Kabbala.

Chapter One offers an alternative metaphor by which we might
reenter the scriptural text. By reading holy literature as if it were
a dream, we gain access to a primary mode of our collective unconscious. The Bible, for us, is an entrance to the cave, perhaps the
only entrance. The great dream of Western religion.

Chapter Two considers this consciousness beneath waking. The
ancient Hebrew literary form known as Midrash, which seeks to
fill in the spaces between the words of Scripture, is analogous to
the psychotherapeutic experience, which likewise seeks to join the
fragments of one's life into a greater unity of meaning. The Eden
legend explains why this underlying consciousness appears only
sporadically, and why our lives are disconnected. Brokenness is
the price of our ability to procreate sexually.

Chapter Three suggests a new understanding of the revelation
in the wilderness. It was a time when humanity, for a moment,
turned its awareness back upon itself, and in so doing understood
its origin and destiny. Western religious tradition is still confused
as to the source of the voice it heard, and continues to insist on
a radical split between public and private spiritual experience. In
the light of a closer biological observation, however, the line between external and internal begins to blur. We participate in a
perpetual organic conversation with our universe. Consciousness
itself may not reside inside our bodies, nor God outside them. In
silence we can hear again the voice issuing from without and
within each of us.

Chapter Four remembers the primordial human form. Not as a
historic myth (i.e., Adam), but as a being in whom we all participate. We are all cells of one organism, and thus biologically inter-
connected with Adam (the first) and the Messiah (the last). All
creation is patterned according to an inner blueprint or arrange-

ment that carries within it a genetic memory of everything that ever happens. Insofar as Scripture is the conscious "alluvium" of the river of light, it can in principle be literally and scientifically true.

Chapter Five suggests how light might be more than merely a metaphor for consciousness. Recent work in astrophysics and cosmology tells of a creation event that is astonishingly parallel to the one described by spiritual tradition. Perhaps light is, in some sense, consciousness pulsing within and unifying all being. This then would be identical with the first creation of the Holy One of Being. The One who seeks to become fully conscious and creates humanity as the "organ" of that yearning.

Chapter Six speaks of the nothingness through which consciousness is transformed. Awareness itself exists on a hierarchy, the levels of which correspond to many of the traditional names for God. The last name for God and Self is nothingness. Only when one is willing to pass through that "sea" can there be redemption and rebirth.

Chapter Seven envisions the possibility of allowing the river of light—the deepest currents of consciousness—to rise to the surface and, without anxiety, animate our lives. We are thus blessed to return to the scriptural text of our ordinary lives and live out its dream. Not to leave life but to learn how to be fully present in it. Such is the promise of the story of Abraham, our father, with which this essay begins. "The Holy One gave a sign to Abraham that everything which happened to him would happen to his children" (*Tanḥumma Lekh Lekha* 9 [Midrash]).


Before we turn to Abraham's journey, a word about the literary genre of this book. Hebrew spiritual tradition has, over the centuries, evolved its own specialized literary mode. Like mystical literature the world over, it is deliberately allusive and esoteric. Much is told but even more is concealed. Not because of any greed on the part of the authors, but because they must surely remember that personal confusion, search, and self-interrogation are more important than any answers could ever be. With the possible exception of the Bible, it is significant that most of this devotional material seems to defy translation. Hebrew is such a distilled language. The vowels are absent and punctuation is sparse. Not uncommonly, one word in Hebrew requires three or four in English. Furthermore, since much of this spiritual literature was originally presented orally, the texts themselves are frequently merely notes. All this only serves to make even the anxious reader go very slowly. Sentences must be reread. Emphases rearranged. Unseen commas and question marks put in place. And still there remains the nagging worry that the text holds another secret, a deeper layer of meaning for a later reading.

It all begins with the Bible itself. Its words are more than holy, they are memento and touchstone for the very formation of the people. Here is a community consecrated to a book. Jewish authors consistently overestimate the people's literacy by punctuating their ideas with fragments of the biblical text. One verse leads to another. These scriptural pieces are the traditionally proper point from which any teacher might venture a new idea. I have tried to continue this tradition.

Midrash, a later literary form, is the writing that sprouts up in the spaces between the consecrated words of Scripture. Somewhere between commentary and fantasy, Midrash imagines super-legends and Ur stories, homily and poetry, emotions and personalities utterly beyond the Bible's words. In one sense, insofar as this essay purports to describe what might "actually" have happened to Abraham, it is itself one long Midrash.

The greatest work of the Jewish mystical tradition is unquestionably the *Zohar*. Claiming itself to be a Midrash on the Five Books of Moses, it is really a compendium of two dozen works, written by Moses de Leon in Spain during the thirteenth century. Whole new mystical ideas are set forth during the course of the wanderings of its purported second-century author, Simeon bar Yochai. A typical page might include a scriptural phrase and a rambling, often highly technical or abstruse series of free associations on its meaning. The reader is given a vision of the inner workings of "God's psyche." Story and outright fantasy alternate with straightforward exposition, all of which converge again on the next biblical phrase to be considered.

The last form that has influenced the idiom of this essay is the Hasidic *sefer,* literally, "religious book." These little texts or manuals are usually the collected table talks, speeches, sermons, or simply *hiddushim* (original interpretations or solutions) of rabbis as "recorded live" by a secretary. The style is intense and assumes a familiarity with prior religious literature.

*The River of Light* draws on this literary tradition. Like midrashic literature in general and the *Zohar* in particular, it is its own contemporary American fantasy-commentary on seven verses from the book of Genesis. It is also, in the mode of the Hasidic *sefer,* an anthology of alternate ways of rendering many classical biblical verses.

Great scholars and poets, many of them of this generation, have set about the sacred task of bringing this literature, together with their own interpretations of it, as the Hebrew idiom puts it, "to light." They are in a real sense those who draw water from the river, and in so doing begin the sacred task of spiritual renewal. It is an honor to add this essay to that collective effort.

I want to thank some of the people who have helped me to chronicle Abraham's journey: Dr. Alan Fisch (psychiatry); Professor Herbert Gursky (cosmology); Professor Norman Hecht (molecular biology); Professor Daniel Matt (*Zohar*); and especially Professor Paul Davidovits (physics), who generously shared their great learning with me. Any errors in this essay are entirely mine. I also want to thank Bette Roth, who was a source of great encouragement; my secretaries, Irma Halperin and Sandra Hall, who—in addition to learning how to read my handwriting—tended this manuscript with great devotion; Marie Cantlon, who nurtured this book; and the members of my congregation, Beth El of the Sudbury River Valley, who patiently endured the sermons and classes that were to become the substance of the following pages.

Above all, I want to thank my wife. It has been Karen's steady faith in the vision of these ideas that has enabled me to make the journey. She is an *ayshet hayil,* a wonderful woman.

*Erev Shabbat,* on which we read,
"And Abraham ran to the herd
and took a calf. . . ."

*Five thousand seven hundred forty-one years
since the creation of the world.
Sudbury, Massachusetts*

L.

*What happens to the parents is already a sign of what will
happen to the children.*—*Sota* 34a (Talmud)[1]

# Abraham's Journey:
# A Legend

Imagine that you are already growing old. And that God has promised that your progeny will be as numerous as the stars of the heavens and the seashore sand. Somehow you will endure years beyond counting. And, somehow, distant galaxies and common bits of earth will be related to you, owe their being to you. As child to parent. Made of the same genetic material. The boundary between now and not yet will softly blur. And the clean line between your discrete body and all creation will someday be no more.

But on that promise God has not delivered. After smashing your father's idols and setting out for a new land and trials too numerous to recount, the covenant promise seems to be a hoax. There is no progeny. Your wife is barren. And because you are older now, the cycle of breathing out and breathing in takes longer than before.

And now you are sitting there at the entrance to your tent. Daydreaming. This is what happened to Abraham according to the first seven verses of Genesis 18:

And the Lord appeared to him by the oaks of Mamre; He was sitting at the entrance of the tent in the heat of the day.

He raised his eyes and looked; and behold, three people were standing by him; and he looked and he ran to meet them from the entrance of the tent; and he bowed to the ground.

And he said, "My lord(s), if I have found favor in your eyes do not pass on by your servant.

Let now a little water be brought and wash your feet and recline under the tree.

I will get a little food and you will refresh yourselves, afterwards you will travel on, since you have come by your servant's way. They said, "Do as you have said."

And Abraham hurried to the tent, to Sarah and he said, "Hurry; three measures of fine flour; knead and make cakes."

And Abraham ran to the herd and he took a calf . . .


According to the scriptural text, the getting of a calf took only a short time and was uneventful. A person gets up from reading a book. Goes to the refrigerator. Gets some food. Returns. The story before us literally says nothing about what may or may not have happened between the time Abraham "ran to the herd" and "took a calf." But just because it says nothing does not mean that nothing happened. After all, preparing lunch for three messengers of Heaven—even if one does not know their origin or mission—is no trivial business. In the few moments of a dream, does it not often seem that an eternity has passed? Is it not at least occasionally the case that we set out on a clear and simple mission and return with something undreamed of? Whether or not we accomplish our original intention becomes unimportant. Abraham, according to the plain meaning of the biblical text, is destined to be the progenitor of the people of Israel. But at this moment he is a "childless patriarch," unaware that after this fateful lunch the promise of progeny will be confirmed. Perhaps there is something more he ought to know. Not another test to be passed or even an experience to be endured, but something to see. Something rather ordinary and mundane. Something seen on the short trip to the kitchen. Here is what midrashic tradition imagines Abraham saw between the time he "ran to the herd" and "took a calf." Think of Abraham as being momentarily blinded by a stray, reflected beam of sunlight. Remember that the Aramaic idiom for one who is blind is *sagi nahor*, "full of light."

"Rabbi Eleazar said, Abraham . . . was running after the calf. . . . But the calf ran away. It entered a cave, and so Abraham followed it and then he saw. . . ."[2]

Another version. "Rabbi Juda said: Abraham . . . [saw] Adam and Eve buried there. He knew that they were Adam and Eve because he saw the form of a person. And while he was gazing, a door opened into the Garden of Eden and he perceived the same form standing near it. Now whoever looks at the form of Adam cannot escape death. For when a person is about to pass out of this world he catches sight of Adam and at that moment he dies. Abraham, however, did look at him, and saw his form and yet survived. He saw moreover, a shining light [a river of light] that illuminated the cave and a lamp burning. Abraham then coveted that cave for his burial place, and his mind and heart were set upon it. . . ."[3]

It is written that "A river issues from Eden . . ." (Gen. 2:10). Now as that river flows out of Eden to water the garden, so from the entrance at the center of the garden emerges a shining river. . . ."[4]

Another version. "When Abraham entered the cave for the first time he saw there a light, and as he advanced, the earth lifted, revealing to him two graves. An image of Adam then arose and, seeing Abraham, smiled at him. Abraham thus knew that this was the place destined for his burial."[5]

In another place. "The Holy One took pity on Adam and when he died allowed him to be buried near the Garden of Eden. For Adam had made a cave near the Garden, and had hidden himself there with his wife. He knew it was near the garden, because he saw a thin ray of light enter it from there, and therefore he desired to be buried in it; and there he was buried, close to the entrance of the Garden of Eden. So it is that a person does not depart from this world until Adam, the first person, appears to him. . . ."[6]

And in another place. "Adam says, The Holy One buried me here, and from that time until now I have been lying here like a frozen seed until you came. . . . Hence it is written, "And the field and the cave that is therein arose . . ." [Gen. 23:17]; in other words, it literally arose before the presence of Abraham, since up to that time nothing there had been visible, but now what had been hidden rose up. . . .' "[7]

Abraham, in other words, thought he was chasing a calf, but instead found his own gravesite. The *Zohar* cannot resist punning on the Hebrew word for calf, *bakar,* which—by transposing the first two letters—reads *kever,* or grave. And all this is the story of how the cave at Machpelah, the ancestral burial place (Gen. 23), was originally found by Abraham.

In setting out in search of "lunch," Abraham found the cave, humanity's parents, the Garden of Eden, and his own ultimate burial place. (Whereupon he returned from the kitchen. "All we have is cheese and some tuna fish salad from last week.") All within the space between "ran to the herd" and "took a calf." Consider, please, that Abraham is not only our father; he is also our story: the Holy One gave a sign to Abraham that everything that happened to him would happen to his children.[8]

Now all these collected fragments and fantasies that sparkle from out of the biblical text form their own coherent super-legend. A discrete story that flows in and out of the superficial biblical story. It tells of an extraordinary journey that Abraham, our father, once made. Of how he once slipped through the "scriptural text" of his daily life into the primordial light of consciousness itself. Into that river of light that nourishes all being. "A river flows out from Eden. . . ."

# Chapter 1

# Like Ones in a Dream

*The ultimate source of a dream may be traceable to tensions, or conditions, or events, antecedent not only to the dream itself but also to the physical organism that occasioned the dream and was its medium—primordial tensions and events which were not produced by, but which produced, the physical organism itself as well as producing the consciousness that is correlative to a physical organism.*

—*Owen Barfield*[1]

*The dream is a . . . plastic manifestation during sleep of an enduring, unconscious "drama" operating continuously, day and night . . . an expression of a more enduring fantasy.*

—*Herbert Fingarette*[2]

*[Raba] said to [the dream interpreter]: I saw two turnip tops. He replied, you will receive two blows with a cudgel. On that day Raba went and sat all day in the academy. He found two blind men quarrelling with one another. Raba went to separate them and they gave him two blows. They wanted to give him another blow but he said, Enough! I saw in my dream only two.*

—*Berachot 56a*[3]

*A consciousness glistens within each creature and each creature's creation, even as it guided the hand of the One who spoke and the world came into being. Rabbi Oshaya, at the beginning of* Genesis Rabba, *reminds us that when even a king builds a castle, he uses a blueprint.[4] So the Creator, too, returns again and again to that underlying pattern of being. Arrangements of motion that organize and animate all being. This is reality's dream. Holy literature. Organizing motif beneath the apparent surface.*

*This consciousness is never still, not even for a moment. It will not be photographed or even named. In its wanting to become aware, it rearranges itself in one pattern after another. Feel it now in the blinking of your eyes. The moisture on your tongue. The gentle filling and emptying of your lungs. It rises unnamed through us, the incessant motion of the four creatures bearing the chariot in Ezekiel's vision: human, lion, ox, and eagle, running and returning. Creation is in us. The plan the Creator used reappears everywhere: from the most erudite contemporary cosmological theory to the opening sentences of Genesis, it is the same.*

*Before we can follow Abraham's journey, we must first meet him in the scriptural text. But this is itself an unknown place. For earlier generations, it was perhaps a place of literal truth and holiness. But now, even for those of us who can recite the words by heart, it is a place on no map. Logically impossible: entirely human and entirely God's word. And, like other holy indescribable places and times, it has a dreamlike quality.*

*"When the Holy One brought us back to Zion, we were like ones in a dream" (Ps. 126:1). Of course, there are many ways to understand the word "dream." Most commonly, it denotes a nocturnal hallucination. Something foggy, surrealistic, and above all, unreal. Another kind of dream speaks of a worked-for, hoped-for future, as in "I have a dream." Here the speaker concedes that the dream is a wish. And then there is the dream that is too good to be true. This is the kind of dream in which the author of Psalm 126 understood the returning exiles to live. Here the wish of the past and the future-now-become-present are the same. An order of being that ever flows beneath and unifies all reality. The great dream. The eternal yearning.*

## HOLY WORDS

No one really knows what dreams are.[5] Hallucinatory wish fulfillment, the voice of the collective unconscious, a continuous process parallel to consciousness,[6] random sorting of overloaded memory circuits, the medium of prophecy, or the mind's struggle to circumvent the formal law of contradiction,[7] no one really knows. But everyone dreams anyway. And we—from Joseph to Daniel to Freud—have had dreams, read them, interpreted them, hidden from them, and even, on occasion, faithfully chanted them from a handwritten parchment scroll. They are an intimate part of our lives.

The Bible is another story. For all its ubiquity and all our devout attention, it remains worlds away. So far away that its sanctity no longer awes; its humanity no longer humbles; the mode of consciousness it might once have evoked no longer possible. What once was the place where humanity and the One of Being might peer into each other's minds, perhaps sharing a moment or two, seems lost. We need a metaphor, an intermediate place between creature and Creator. Ironically, even though the Bible itself is precisely that metaphor, we continue to search elsewhere.

In our own day, several metaphors enjoy a wide currency. Each one has its own insight and clarifies another dimension of a mode of consciousness that, finally, can have no direct expression. We say that Scripture is like great religious literature. But that removes the possibility of its holiness, and consequently undermines the worth of any particular religion's tradition of understanding the biblical text. Some have suggested that the Bible is like a marriage contract. This recovers some of the holiness and intimacy, but ultimately fails, inasmuch as no one religiously studies the terms of a marriage. Or we say that the Bible is like history or archaeology or culture; in this way we may learn history or archaeology or culture, but not Bible. Or we say that the Bible is like an anthology of ethical teachings; unfortunately, many of the Bible's obvious ethical teachings are patently unacceptable. Sometimes we give in to that precious nagging human need for a higher authority and side with orthodox fundamentalist tradition in claiming that the whole thing is simply, literally true and that the Holy One of Being wrote it word for word. But by insisting on such a crystalline reading of what are inescapably human words, we only make a travesty of the holy lights they must obviously conceal. There is even a metaphor in which we liken ourselves to the pious ones of old. This works as long as we can go on pretending. And so it is that we spend most of our time not learning Bible, but apologizing for it, becoming servants of our own metaphors.

We seek a metaphor for holy words that will return them to us once again as an *aytz ḥayim,* a tree of life (Prov. 3:18). One that yields heightened self-awareness *and* God's Word. One that permits sustained intellectual inquiry *and* Scripture's holiness. One that preserves clarity, but not at the expense of mystery. One whose playfulness does not dilute piety. One whose public objectivity tolerates personal intimacy. In the spiritual code words of our generation: a holy text.


## THE GREAT DREAM

If a group of people can have a psyche and think of itself as an organic being, then surely a people should also be able to dream. A series of motifs and archetypes should keep reappearing and seem to each individual dreamer, as Jung suggested, to emanate from a transcendent source.[8] God would be present in those dreams, even as God speaks to and is within the people themselves. Johannes Pedersen, the Danish Bible scholar, in describing the biblical mind—our group mind of an earlier time—observes that, while "the dream is a communication from God to man . . . it does not clash with the psychological process. The dream is a communication from God because it is a direct outcome of reality itself."[9]

And this is how it goes. In each generation there are encounters with the Holy Ancient One of Old. Visioned and recorded almost unconsciously. And some encounters, by reason of their terror or subtlety, simply go unrecorded. Fragments remembered the next morning at breakfast. Slid through the cracks. Finding their way to the dream-memory of the people. And then it happens that one of the people writes, sings, legislates, scolds, or simply remembers. Perhaps with some awareness of destiny, or maybe just to earn a living. No matter. Each is organically part of us, an instrument of the Word. And their collective bringing-to-our-attention is the great dream.

14

Scripture, then, might be understood as what has been saved for us of our collective memory. A remnant of the work of ten thousand censors. And several dozen poets, prophets, and teachers. The last of these may have been our parents (who read the Bible to us, although perhaps with a different intention). A kind of journal of forgotten, reworked, and remembered holy moments, too awesome to be simply described in everyday conscious language. It is all that remains of the most penetrating incursion of waking into the earth-mother-Jewish-people darkness of what is not the spirit, but only sleep. But the memory is still there, set in our bodies by our parents or our choice.

We may ignore the dream or we may appropriate it for ourselves, and so make it our own. It is our choice alone.

Scripture is the result of the attempt to bring to the lifelight of consciousness the latent, unresolvable dialectic of unconsciousness. The left cerebral hemisphere's futile foray into the right side. Rational language's hopeless try at putting in a simple proposition what can only be said in a disjunctive one. Or, as it is told that Abraham Joshua Heschel taught about all holy stories, "An occasion when the heart surprises the mind."

Now this common dream is more than a mythic belief system: it is part of our very being.[10] And this, then, is the job of the searchers and the dreamers: to reach deeper and deeper into the dream. Peeling away one layer after another. Until we realize that the voice speaking our dreams comes from within us and from without at the same time.[11] Until we see at last that the story is true. Not necessarily because it happened in a particular place at a particular time, but because it is within us. It always was. It issues from us. It is ours. The whole ancient hierarchy of meanings. Each word is a *PaRDeS,* an orchard of four possibilities. *Peshat:* the simple meaning, literal, superficial, waking. *Remez:* the hinted meaning, allegorical, concealed, dreaming. *Drash:* the interpreted meaning, searched, learned, unconscious. *Sod:* the secret meaning, mystical, universal, transpersonal, infinite. Confusion. Mystery.

Terror and light. The whole thing. All belongs to us. It is something we know from our innermost being. Even as it echoes the One who spoke the first letter that had no sound. It is our dream. It is a holy text. And this dream bears a remarkable similarity to time-honored notions of Bible.

Both Bible and dream are first encountered as mystery, and in the final interpretation remain mystery. For both are inexhaustible and infinitely analyzable. "It is a fragment of a dream we get under all circumstances."[12]

Both Bible and dream are multi-layered. Intelligible as the manifest *peshat* simple shell of the fruit. And yet, upon closer observation, concealing a myriad of deeper layers. Each one somehow protecting the latent *sod* secret seed within.

Both Bible and dream create their own internal logic and systems of space and time. There is no before or after in the Torah.[13]

In both Bible and dream, nothing is accidental. The most trivial detail or the most nonsensical pun is there for a reason.

In both Bible and dream the story and the characters and even the very words and letters themselves are contorted, convoluted, condensed, inverted, rearranged, and often out of place. But we do not dismiss such a dream.

Both Bible and dream are creations from the innermost depths of our collective and individual beings. Creations of our ancient memories of holy history that seem to hint at the ultimate nature of reality.

Both Bible and dreams seem to issue from outside ourselves. Whether from the collective memory, or (as Zalman Schachter Shalomi suggested) "A letter we have written to ourselves from some previous incarnation," or the word of God.

Both Bible and dream, in moments of understanding, seem to come from inside us. Some thin, barely audible sound of almost breathing (1 Kings 19:12), a way each of us has of talking with ourselves privately. Whether Freud's hallucinatory wish fulfillment or the voice of religious inspiration.

16

And both Bible and dream share an ability to synthesize the external, communal, and public dimension of life with its internal, private, and personal side. Indeed, from Jung to Freud, or from mystic to rationalist, both Bible and dream are understood by parallel spectra of interpretations.

## THE INTERPRETATION OF SCRIPTURE AND OTHER DREAMS

Suppose Scripture were like a dream, and we were its vessels. Likes ones in a dream. If Scripture be like a dream, then methods of understanding the dream are, at least in principle, valid for learning Scripture. Let us consider some of the modes of dream interpretation. Ten classic entrances to the dream. Ten ways of considering our own conscious spiritual creation. For, by understanding our dream, we understand more than Scripture. We understand ourselves.

1. Begin with the most difficult and subtle question of all. One that will flow through successive answers as our own self-awareness deepens: what is the underlying emotional dynamic of the story? "The emotions displayed in the dream are its most reliable elements. The emotion usually corresponds to the latent but not always to the manifest content of the dream."[14] When viewed from a distance, what is the feel of the dream's prevailing emotion? What holds it together? Keeps our interest? *In the Abraham story, who are the strangers? Will Abraham (we) catch the calf? What is in the cave? Then fear and awe: will Abraham (we) die? Humility: here is where he (we) wishes to be buried.*

2. Recall our own recent, immediate experiences. Since dreams are often initiated by something that happened only recently, we must ask about yesterday's residue. What were the extraordinary

events that startled our consciousnesses and thereby sparked the dream? *Abraham—the text implies and other sources are convinced*[15]*—has just finalized his end of the covenant by circumcising himself, his son Ishmael and his entire household* (Gen. 17:23–7). *At the age of ninety-nine, he has (after his son is born!) put the mark of the deal on his own organ of regeneration. And he is now sitting at the door of the tent . . .*

3. Isolate and identify the primary elements of the dream text before us. What are the dream's components? One of the most common errors made in trying to understand a dream is the almost automatic refusal to recognize more than one character or element or verbal idea in the narrative, when of course, all the parts are indispensable. *Not only Abraham and Sarah and the travelers, but the calf and the cave and the light at its other end. Not only welcoming and searching and exploring, but chasing and flight and discovery.*

4. Pay especially close attention to the seemingly trivial details and the little discrepancies. If teachers and interpreters who preceded us were unafraid to seek significance in puns, letter arrangement, or even the tiny crownlets of the ancient Hebrew script, then neither should we. It is often the case that some seemingly trivial word conceals the entrance to a deeper meaning. *The messengers were literally "people" (not angels), and they were not approaching. When he looked up they were already standing there. Surely only one messenger is needed for a message. So why are there three? One to bring the "good news" to Sarah. One to overthrow Sodom. One to heal Abraham.* [16]

5. We must not allow embarrassment to distract attention from elements that make us uncomfortable. Disgust and dread are the sorts of feelings we frequently marshal to conceal deeper layers of our psyche. "If an element appearing in a myth or in a dream belongs to a much earlier phase of development and is not part of the conscious frame of reference at the time of the final formation of the myth, this element often carries with it the quality of dread

and awefulness."[17] "*And while Abraham was gazing, a door opened into the Garden of Eden and he perceived the same form standing near it. . . .*"[18]

6. If this Scripture dream is actually ours, then our associations are also relevant. Often, they will obviously be of only personal validity, but at other times they will open new dimensions of understanding as compelling as those of commentators of old. What first occurs to us on remembering the dream/reading the text may be the most important thing. The key itself. *The story is rich with procreation imagery. Abraham circumcised. God has promised progeny. Three messengers corresponding to the three of the male genitalia. Abraham "enters" the tent/his wife. Enters the cave/earth/womb. Finds his own parents. . . .*

7. Assume full responsibility for the dream. For "through the dream the man makes the matter his own; it is in his will, and he is responsible for it."[19] We usually hide from our dreams by thinking of ourselves as passive movie screens upon which they are shown. We refuse to believe that they are our own meticulous creations, which we as individual dreamers or heirs of a particular spiritual tradition have authored. But to place anything in the scripture/dream outside ourselves is only to align ourselves with the wicked son of the *Haggadah*'s Passover story, who denies any part in the tale. If the dream is confused, then it is we who have confused it. "The teaching of God is complete" (Ps. 19:87). That is, it is in the form it is supposed to be. If the dream has an evil side, then it is also a side of us. We are responsible for the evil impulses of our dreams.[20] *We set Abraham at the entrance of the tent. Sent him three wayfarers. Had him decide to slaughter a calf. Had the calf run away. . . .*

8. The dream can condense opposites into one truth. "Dreams show a special tendency to reduce two opposites to a unity. . . . Anything in a dream may mean its opposite. . . . We must therefore

entertain the hypothesis that there is an important connection between being 'dialectical' and dreaming, just as there is between dreaming and poetry or mysticism."[21] *Abraham does not enter a cave; he turns into himself. Adam and Eve and the Garden with its light are already within his bones. Perhaps the calf is something within each of us that convinces us to take another path.*

9. The many selves, who together comprise one self, often separate. They stand before us in stark relief. Our selves have many facets. We must therefore be all the parts of our dream. If the Scripture dream is ours, then we have done more than "have it," we have made it. Everything in it comes from us. Each character. Each scene. Each object. We chose them. Wrote the lines, or at least recorded them and not others. Abraham and Ur. Sacrifices and Sinai and blood and God and Moses and, yes, even Pharaoh. As he appears to us in our dream, he is our creation. We made him. For indeed he, too, is in us. As any good teacher of dreams will tell you, you are all the people in your dream. Fritz Perls taught, "[All] the different parts, any part in the dream—is yourself, is a projection of yourself."[22] And to ask why we made our story this way and not that way is to reenter our sacred text once again as living participants. We could have made it another way, but chose to cast it in this one. We must be all the parts of our dream, even the ones we don't like. *The Abraham who chases animals and sons in order to slaughter them is also us. Part of ourselves.*

10. Through the dream/Scripture we slip back to our origins. Through that infinity of meanings we return to the undifferentiatedness of all existence. Another earlier (perhaps earliest) order of being, which not only punctuates our sleep but (we intuit) continuously flows beneath waking. "The feeling of oneness with the universe, the ability of all contents to change shape and place, in accordance with the laws of similarity and symbolic affinity, the symbolic character of the world, and the symbolic meaning of all

spatial dimensions—high and low, left and right, etc.—the significance of colors, and so forth, all this the world of dreams shares
with the dawn period of mankind."[23] This is the great dream of
which each individual dream is a personal manifestation. Dream
is ontogenetic. Myth is phylogenetic. "Dreams and especially
myths are a primary medium for intuitive insights into the ultimate nature of human existence . . . [they] are not restricted to
. . . sleep. They pertain rather to the symbolic dimension of human
experience as a whole."[24] *Abraham lives. Welcomes messengers. Follows
a calf. Discovers a cave. Finds parents, light, paradise, and makes lunch. This
minute. Now. In us.*

## TO LIVE IN THE DREAM

And then we awake to discover that the dreams we have
dreamed are none other than the lives we live. In the words of the
prophet Nathan (scolding David, the king—who has just been told
an allegory of his life): "Thou art the man!" (2 Sam. 12:7). The
story is not about someone else. It is not even about you. It *is* you.
The one who "lives" in the dream is the one who dreams. Just as
the dream softly pulses beneath everyday waking—noticeable
only when the din and clatter of daytime is stilled by sleep—so the
one who remembers a dream brings a new facet to waking.
"The dreamer," wrote philosopher Herbert Fingarette," . . . must
. . . experience the reality of his secret life. . . ."[25] We must live
in and through and out our dreams. Live in and through and out
the great dream of being. Not, of course, in the way we speak of
a man who lives in a dream, meaning that he inhabits an interior
world of his own creation, that his life is hopelessly invested in
some escapist fantasy, or that his only hope is some imaginary
future, which he knows in his heart of hearts will never be realized. To live in the dream means that what Abraham once did is
also for us to do. "What happens to the parents is already a sign

of what will happen to the children"[26] Abraham welcomes unknown angels in us. We chance upon the cave at Machpelah in our
lives. And we find its Eden entrance at the other end.

To live in the dream means that what we "created" last night
is not something other than this morning's waking life, but a
subterranean part of it. The final function of mythology "is to
initiate the individual into the orders of his own psyche, guiding
him toward his own spiritual enrichment and realization."[27]

To live through the dream means that what Abraham left un-
done might still be realized through our actions. And that what we
witnessed last night is a truth we are trying to tell ourselves about
ourselves, but are yet afraid to utter in the morning.

To live out the dream means that what Abraham could not even
imagine, we can see. The dream/myth of centuries and its personalized appearance during nighttimes is not immutable. And we are
not its puppets.

We made the dream. We wrote, are writing, and will rewrite
again its lines. Shifting its selves and plots and scenery and se-
quences in accordance with our abilities to endure awareness. We
may, if we choose, be present in a world of constant commerce
with the dream. To the extent that we can take responsibility for
our unconscious dream lives, we are permitted to participate in
their creation.

The dream is not static. Not something "out there." It has no
fixed script, nor even a permanent past. It is constantly in motion.
Perpetually flowing from us, just as our consciousness is never
still. To utter the dream is to interpret it. And to interpret it is to
change it. When we put into words something that did not happen
in words, we give it a new and seemingly fixed image. Yet from
day to day even the words themselves acquire new shades and
subtleties. And to think about their meanings, so as to get a clearer
understanding of them, is to step onto the dance floor before the
music has stopped. The dream is never still. It is infinitely analyzable, until finally, into that infinity of meanings, all the universe is

drawn. Through the dream we enter into a relation with a hitherto unmet facet of being. As Freud said of our dream lives, "They are not only in me but act 'from out of me as well.' "[28]

Perhaps there is another sense in which the dream creates us. The totality of all the dreams that have been dreamed or are yet to be, whether understood or even remembered, work through us, with or without our individual or collective consent. With or without our knowledge. This consciousness, toward which we journey, flowing softly beneath everything, animating and filling our substance, speaks through us. And it joins us with all creation.

The one who pays attention to the dreams, draws on them, and lives them out is blessed, even as the one who dreams is also dreamt. We each take our turn at living out the dream. Like some ageless wave, Scripture flows through us.


Not long ago, we dreamt the Bible. From deep within our several and collective unconsciousnesses, we brought it forth. Twisted, convoluted, and mysterious. But nevertheless true beyond our wildest dreams. Unable to withstand the going up from our depths, enough to remain in simple *peshat* form, it cloaked itself in mystery,[29] transformed intolerable desires into dense imagery and words, deleted the "good parts," substituting them with parts that seemed "good." Now all we have left is the piously handed down scroll, filled with square black letters, the spaces between them, and, of course, our own fragmented memories of a dream.

"Amemar, Mar Zutra and Rab Ashi would say this. *Ribono shel Olam,* Holy One of Being, *Ani shelcha v'halomoti shelcha,* I am yours and my dreams are yours. *Halom halamti,* I have dreamed a dream. *V'ay-nehni yodea mah hu* and I do not know what it means. . . ."[30]

# Chapter 2

# The River
# of Light

*Each person is at each moment capable of remembering all that has ever happened to him and of perceiving everything that is happening everywhere in the universe. The function of the brain and nervous system is to protect us from being overwhelmed and confused by this mass of largely useless and irrelevant knowledge, by shutting out most of what we should otherwise perceive or remember at any moment, and leaving only that very small and special selection which is likely to be practically useful."*

*—Aldous Huxley [1]*


*It is written in Genesis (2:10), "A river went forth from Eden." . . . It is also written in Jeremiah (17:8), "For he shall be as a tree planted by the waters, that spreads forth its roots by the river." In the book of Rab Hamnuna the elder it is called "Life," because life issues from there into the world. . . . We have also laid down that the great and mighty tree in which is food for all is called the Tree of Life, because its roots are in that Life. . . . We have learned that that river sends forth deep streams . . . to water the Garden and feed the trees and the shoots. . . .*

*—Zohar [2]*

26

*There is a realm of being that comes before us and follows after us. Streaming through and uniting all creation. Knowing who we have been and will be. It contaminates our sleep with visions of higher reality and exalts our waking with stories. It is a river of light. "She is a tree of Life to those who hold on to her" (Prov. 3:18). Her branches and shoots are the nerves and vessels of this world coursing beneath our surfaces, pulsing through our veins. A blueprint underlying the cosmos. The primary process of being. The inner structure of consciousness. The way of the Tao. "And all her paths are peace" (Prov. 3:17). Just behind and beneath everything. If we could but stand it, everything would have meaning. Everything connected to everything else even as they all share a common Root.*

*Once a dream is told, it becomes something else. No sooner has it been recorded or told or even remembered than it ceases to be a dream. Now it is part of waking, it is torn from what shines beneath it and bore it, no longer part of the totality, only a story, perhaps. Waking consciousness closes out more than it lets in. It is said of one rabbi that he had to put on glasses in order to limit his vision. And philosopher Henri Bergson suggested that the main task of our sensory apparatus* is not productive, but eliminative. [3] In the same way, what you describe as a dream is often only a small part of the dream. It is only a piece. The remembered dream, in its manifest, apparent, peshat, simple meaning, is at best only a collection of fragments. Condensed. Rearranged. Symbolic. Unintelligible. Preposterous. Fantastic. Frightening because of its terrible and urgent importance.

Abraham might say: "I dreamt that I went to the herd to get lunch and that I returned." Is that all? Does anything else come to mind? (Or the simply less directive, "Oh?") "Why yes. Now that I think of it, there was this one calf that I selected, but it ran away. Of course! I remember." (We might also say, Why don't you invent some story? It would have the same importance.) "I must have chased that dumb animal (never even suspecting I was being lead) off into the fields. And damned if it didn't disappear into a cave. One I had never seen. Deep hollow mysterious darkness. Alice in Wonderland. Earth mother womb. My past. Another dimension of my psyche. Another layer of consciousness. A past. A future. Full of parents and death and life and light. What a place. . . ."

## MIDRASH AND MEANING

Scripture says only that Abraham went to the herd, got a calf, and returned. It does not say or even suggest that he chased one into a cave, discovered Adam and Eve, and found the Garden of Eden. In no way can it be inferred from the narrative. This deliberate leaving of the text of the "remembered dream," creating a story and returning to the next word, is called, in Hebrew, Midrash. Not the creation of a story from out of thin air, which is called "fantasy." Nor the elaboration of one word or event and returning to this same word or event, which is called "commentary." But the deliberate filling in of the gap between two words. Not to dissolve their individuality, but to fuse them into the even greater totality from which they have risen and of which they are only a part. This is called Midrash.

An example of another Midrash: Later on in Genesis, Abraham is told to sacrifice Isaac. After a three-day journey, "Abraham looked up and saw the place from afar. Then Abraham said to his servants, 'You stay here with the donkey. . . .' " (Gen. 22:4–5). Between the time he "saw the place from afar" and his directions to his servants, there is a Midrash.

What did Abraham see when he looked up? The cloud of God's presence on the mountain. Turning to Isaac, he said, "Do you see it too, my son?" "Yes, my father, I see it too." Then he turned to the two servants. "Do you see it?" "No," they said, "we don't see anything." "Then in that case," Abraham replied to his servants, "You stay here with the donkey, because he doesn't see anything either!"[4]

Midrash, then, is a literature that appears in the spaces in between. After one word is done but before the next one has opened its mouth. It is a unique literary form, as Rabbi Arnold Wieder has taught, having as its necessary prerequisite a consecrated text. It tells a story that has as its beginning a word in the scriptural text and returns, upon its completion, to the next word in the manifest story. And even though what it describes may have literally nothing to do with the scriptural narrative, it nevertheless requires a foreknowledge of that narrative for its aesthetic and spiritual power. The poet Joel Rosenberg has gone on to suggest that Scripture itself is a form of Midrash but, alas, we have lost the Ur text for Scripture. We are in possession not of the dream itself, but only of its next-morning memory. Once a dream is told, it becomes something else.

To fill in the spaces between the words. Is this not the task of all who would be whole? Not just creating stories to connect the fragments of a dream or Scripture, but of life also. Somehow, between the time we were children and this time, we have forgotten how to connect "little" events in our past with "little" things nowadays. What happened between the first parents and ourselves? We have misplaced the story that connects the past and the present. Scripture is only an incomplete record. Our memories and dreams are no better. And so the process of Midrash and the process of therapy are analagous. Health, like real understanding of Scripture, will occur at a time when the spaces are filled in. When the beginning of the story is meaningfully and honestly joined with the end. When we can see them once again within the river whence they have come.

Health (to heal, to make whole) is the result of connecting the discordant and apparently unrelated pieces. And illness is pretending (or believing) that what is broken is really whole: something happens. Stop. A while later (hours or days or years) we do something else. Stop. But because we do not perceive our actions as responses to previous events, this action is unintelligible. It is part of no greater system of meaning. Our lives seem to be ruled by the caprice of distant, uncaring powers. Our joy is irrelevant. And our grief is unbearable. On the other hand, if we can create a story connecting one "fragment" of our lives with another and thus join with Midrash-gossamerlike webs those separate fragments of our existence, there is now a sentence where before there were only words. Meaning is literally in the connections. And meaninglessness obtains when the events in our lives seem to us unrelated, discordant, and fragmentary. (And what shall we say to the one whose midrashim/stories are delusionary? Only that their stories do not begin or end with the common text before us all.)

We are able to distinguish between four levels of awareness that correspond to the apparent connectedness of the events of our lives. At the first level, nothing seems connected to anything else. Events and actions and plans stream along without any apparent plan. We feel like debris floating in a flood. We spot a goal floating over there and swim toward it. We might make it. We might fail. We give up. We forget it. Something else floats by. Abraham discovers three wayfarers. He goes to the herd to get a calf. So it goes.

At the second level, we find ourselves surprised by what "seems" to float before us. Goals we had sought seem suddenly within our reach. Larger segments of our lives seem now connected. Guided along by some unseen current. We say, "Things are working out the right way," or "It's as if 'someone' is taking care of me." We are amazed and grateful. Abraham follows the calf. He is willing to follow the thread of his life wherever it leads. Able temporarily to suspend judgment. Able to be surprised.

Above this level we discover that we are, all the time, with even our most trivial actions and ideas, planting seeds and making arrangements for the future. Everything that we choose to do may affect our course. We are not incapacitated or encumbered by such a realization, for we are not self-conscious. We are, rather, simply aware and above all willing to assume responsibility for whatever we do and whoever we are. Trusting our own unconscious mechanisms and sensing their mysterious relationship with the currents that bear us along. Our lives now have their own inner continuity and meaning. Abraham now understands that he has *chosen* to follow the calf. That he is able to see this cave, which he may have passed by many times before. That he is ready to enter it and participate in the unfolding of his own destiny.

On the highest level, we see our lives and our decisions as being part of a great network that includes the lives and decisions and unconscious intentions of everyone (and everything) with whom we are in perpetual commerce. Now there is a kind of effortlessness and grace with which we do whatever we do. There are no ulterior motives, for every ulterior motive is the primary motive. And this plan is now apparent. It is not a flood but an ocean. Our awareness endures within it. Our awareness sustains it. Abraham understands that the three wayfarers were "sent." That it is up to him to find and see what he finds and sees. And that just as he now knows about Adam and Eve and paradise and his own future burial place, so too they must have known about him all along. He now sees how he is part of the great chain of the generations. In this way the first is joined to the last.

If Scripture is like a dream, then Midrash is like therapy. It is the creative process whereby some of what is concealed is brought to the light of awareness. It is the act of filling in the spaces between the paragraphs and words and letters of the Bible in such a way as to make one long intelligible word, which (according to Kabbalistic tradition) will be the Name of God. The *Shaym Ha-Vayah*, the Name of Being. It is the act of joining the broken and superficially discordant parts of a personality into a meaningful whole. Replacing illness with health. It is therefore also the work of bringing the Messiah.

Midrash, like therapy, does not seek to change the text. Rather, by joining its fragments together in a new and more coherent pattern of meaning, it seeks to set it free of old, paralyzing stereotypes. We open our eyes to the words/personality before us and see it as a new creation. As if it were born just this moment. And while the Midrash (joining this word to that phrase) or the therapeutic interpretation (joining this way of acting to that event) is certainly new, the primary elements remain as they have always been. Only here, now, there is freedom, where before there was only repetition, predictability, and slavery. Indeed, this formal literary tradition by which a holy text is interpreted or reinterpreted might once have served the same vital social and psychological function now tended by psychotherapy.

## PSYCHOTHERAPY AND MYSTICISM

Psychotherapy and mysticism share more than this preoccupation with filling in the blank spaces between life's words. They both reverence the dream. It is the "royal road to the unconscious," a vision set into us from a higher world. And both therapy and mysticism share the same messiannic plan: to heal. To make what was once whole and is now broken, whole again. Indeed, the experiences of the patient and the searcher, as portrayed in the ideal, are so similar that it is hardly surprising that classical mysticism has made such a poor showing in the contemporary West. After all, it makes little difference which of two parallel paths people take to reach the same destination.

Both therapy and mysticism begin by redirecting attention to the one who asks the question. The beginning of the answer is not "out there" but "in here." In the very consciousness of the one who is looking. Our transformation and healing will commence only with sustained introspection. This world before us is not going to change. According to one tradition, a sure test for any would-be rebbe (or guru or spiritual guide—or therapist) is to ask if he has a way to outwit our libidinous impulse. If he says he does, then he is a fake. In a similar way, Freud would speak of transforming hysterical misery into ordinary everyday unhappiness. Only magicians and charlatans claim to be able to change this world. Genuine therapists and mystics claim instead to change the self-awareness of the one who looks and thereby change that person's reality. This world is not going to change. Yes, it is teeming with mysterious powers and miracles, but to seek to manipulate them without first understanding oneself has, for centuries, been known as illness. Only people change. And you are the only one who can change yourself. "God helps those who help themselves." Act therefore as if there were no God. And that will change the world.

The result of this introspection for both therapy and mysticism is always the same. There are within and beyond the self hidden orders of being. "As above, so below."[5] Consciousness is layered. Concealed strata of reality that are inaccessible to ordinary perception. They are literally meta-physical. Freud's genius was evident in his ability to convince scientists of the existence of an unconscious realm for which there could never be conclusive empirical proof. (How ironic that the man who gave Western materialism scientific permission to speak of fantasy should be condemned as a materialist.) This unconscious hidden universe has no place in the world. "Just as the Holy One sees but is not seen, so the soul sees but is not itself seen. . . . Just as the Holy One dwells in the innermost chambers, so the soul abides in the innermost chambers."[6] It is a place that is always deeper. Where the law of contradiction does not apply. Where, as Rabbi Dov Baer of Mezritch taught, "Life and death, sea and dry land are the same."[7] It was once experienced. Now it has been forgotten.

This other dimension is not merely concealed, it flows softly beneath the surface of everything. It moves beneath what is apparent and animates it. It fills this world with "undreamed of" potential meaning, for since it is beneath everything, it joins everything. It is an untamed primeval motion of ever-rearranging arrangements of only God knows what. A primary process that seems to sparkle through ordinary things and events in moments of great insight, beauty, and genius. It is reflected sunlight on water. The dancer who dances with such intensity that self-consciousness is left behind. The musicians in the orchestra who play with such devotion that their combined music is greater than the sum of their individual contributions. One body that joins with another body to form, for a moment, what seems to be a single living organism. When all things around us seem to "flow" within and by the same current. When the words of prayer seem to take wings. Then have we fallen (or risen) beneath the apparent surface to some more primary process. Symbols have greater life. Linear logic recedes. The boundaries of space and time blur. The primeval and archaic return. The dream awakens even though the one who dreams remains asleep.

This is the mother of what we know as consciousness. For both therapy and mysticism, darkness, unconsciousness, primary process, and dream come before light, consciousness, linear logic, and waking. "In the beginning, consciousness rises up like an island, with whatever contents it then has, but soon sinks back again into the unconscious."[8] The darkness is frightening (we can't see in the dark), but it is not evil. Without the dark womb of sleep there could be no sensation of light, emergence of consciousness, or place to which we might return. In the darkness there is no arrangement of past and future, no self-reflection, no ego, and no neurosis. The Talmud teaches that the days of our lives properly begin with darkness and move to daylight.[9] And thus all genuine creating must originate in the darkness. All transformation must commence during the night. At the price of the "old ego" and its organization. You cannot predict what will happen in the darkness.

Now there is a paradox in this image of darkness, unconsciousness, and self, for it is precisely from these ways of being that humanity senses a source of the greatest light. How could the brightest light come from the darkness? Why would it not come from the sun? On the winter solstice, the day of the longest night, whether with a candle on an evergreen tree or a candelabrum, humanity celebrates light. Perhaps we are reassuring ourselves that the days will get no shorter, that this happens every year, and that there is nothing to get very worried about. But perhaps we are reminding ourselves—as we do with all rituals—of a truth long buried. That from the very bottom of the cave there flows a river of light.

There are, of course, other reliable windows to "darker" orders of consciousness. For both therapy and mysticism our deliberate, patient, and undivided attention is a great tool. In one way or another, all the disciplines seem to agree on this need for single-ness of purpose. Direction. Focus. And each tradition in its own way offers techniques for slipping through, beyond, and beneath the control of daily ego wakefulness and predictability. Ways of censoring the censor. Strategies that aim to lull, mesmerize, or outright trick the mechanism of consciousness, whose job seems to be to keep us alive in "this" world (and out of the river). Some have suggested a continuous interruption of the left cerebral hemi-sphere's concern with grammar and syntax is common to all reli-gions.[10] "Look at this." "Consider that." "Imagine the sound of one hand clapping." "Chant a wordless melody *(niggun)* long enough, through the other side of boredom," say the Hasidim, "to the ecstasy beyond."

The rubric of Jewish prayer is the blessing, or *beracha.* They all begin the same way: "Holy One of Blessing, Your Presence fills creation. . . ."[11] An observant traditional Jew might find reason to say scores of them each day. One tradition even says that there are one hundred. Before rising. Before washing one's hands. Before eating. Their real function might be to get us to stop. To pay attention to the holy potential in even our most mundane daily acts.

The therapist says, "Do you see what you're saying? Listen to yourself." Pay attention to each thought. The ones you cus-tomarily censor. (Abraham did not give up on the runaway calf. He ran after it. Stayed with it when he could have chosen another one.) Even free association, which seems to be unfocused, allows us to pay close attention to the very flow of our thinking. To the sequence and arrangement of thoughts occasioned by any (ran-dom) first thought.

And then, in both therapy and mysticism, something strange happens. This deliberate and intense self-attention gives way to unself-consciousness. We cease, in an important and graceful way, to be aware of ourselves. Returned, as it were, to our lives. Our illness, our banishment, our brokenness turn out to have been the result of this deliberate self-reflection of consciousness. But we see that, up until now, it has been incomplete. Until now our attempts at self-understanding have been flawed. Until now we have only had a part of the picture. And our neuroses and our "religions" have been symptoms of this. Instead of fleeing from or trying to conceal these "strange" behaviors, we should have paid even closer attention to them. Done them, as it were, with *kavanah,* devotion. Not to give in to them but to understand them to their very roots. In this way must we seek out the origins of (this most recent layer of) our psyches.

It is no coincidence that Abraham finds humanity's mother and father in that cave. Just as our relationship to our parents, those most recent embodiments of Adam and Eve, color all subsequent relationships and understanding, so must it therefore precede any kind of lasting health or spiritual awareness. Psychotherapy and mysticism agree. Not only have one man and one woman given us life, they have, through malice, ignorance, design, and love, shaped our psyches. Thus, any path back to the One of Being must lead through them. "You shall honor your father and your mother . . . " (Exod. 20:12), for they are the ones through whom you learned to see whatever reality you have. See into and reexperience the story by which your psyche came to be. Look on while the lines of the script are being written. It is an unending and inescapable task. The commandment to honor our parents is the hardest of them all. But only then will our relationships with those around us be transparent to us. And only then will our desire to be good be within our reach. This is the proper and the only sequence. The commandments concerning relationships between one human being and another always take precedence over spiritual awareness. Not because one is more important than the other, but because people are the only path we have. And our parents are our "first" people.

They are our link to the chain of generations' truth. Through them we are able to look backwards. Those "old ones," long gone, turn out to be wiser and more powerful dead than alive. For both psychotherapy and spiritual search, what is earlier is more important than what is later. Unconscious thoughts, repressed and out of sight, exert more force than those that have risen to the surface. It is what we once saw, imagined, planned, did, and knew as a child but have now forgotten that can free us. Indeed, it is from their very hiddenness that they derive their immense power. The force of any secret to control human transactions is well known. We do not know who we are until we "remember" who our parents were. And their parents before them. Our self-awareness is incomplete as long as there is a secret between ourselves and Adam. Now you are right to ask how anyone could possibly know so much. Where could one even begin to search out such an uninterrupted line? The answer, of course, is that this Scripture/dream of ours conceals it all. Turn it and turn it again. Everything is contained therein.[12]

Everything was once known. Only now forgotten. The embryo is shown the primordial light in which all the past and future generations are visible. By which anything is possible and everything known. And then, just before birth, during a scuffle with the angel, we "forget" it all. Born empty.

And before this, before the first parents and the first light, nothing can be known. The ultimate Name of God in the Kabbala is *Ayn Sof*—without end. Utter nothingness. Freud also understood that "in the last analysis the real nature of the unconscious process is a shrouded secret, unknowable, it is something of which we are totally unable to form a conception."[13] Certainly the joining of this world with the river of light beneath it, like the bringing into waking the hidden dream, is the messianic goal of both religion and therapy. But to do so we must return to the source of the river as generations have faithfully preserved it. All the way back.

Abraham notices that the cave is mysteriously filled with light. It looks familiar to him. A river issues from Eden.

There is something that flows beneath this realm. Customarily envisioned as darkness or unconsciousness and feared, it is also a great flowing light. Even brighter than the sunlight of consciousness. Humanity's mythos is the dream memory of this other consciousness, which permeates all being. Independent of living protoplasm. Softly hovering over the surface of the waters. We need only to listen to ourselves and the stories of the old ones, which effortlessly issue from our mouths. Listen very carefully. Follow the calf back to the cave. Notice the reflected light on the surface of water. Realize that the light is not reflected after all. The light was shining through from deep inside the water. Eden, you might say, is not distant in time or even in space.


## AMNESIA OF EDEN

Eden tells everything. Not merely why men must sweat for their bread or women cry out as they bring forth children. It tells also of the tear in the relationship between the children who play in the garden and the parents who are in heaven. It tells further why we (children) are no longer there. And about how sexual maturity, banishment, procreation, and mortality are facets of one totality. It tells of the origin of neurosis. The original sin question, in one sense, means that each child, by virtue of its humanity, is doomed to do again what its parents did to their parents. And, possibly, that it was this very act of primeval disobedience that initiated the inescapable circle of teaching and rebellion. There are lessons that each generation is convinced it must learn for itself, even though it is mistaken. Each generation believes that to listen to its parents would constitute the ultimate act of existential cowardice. To disobey them would mean self-creation, banishment, mortality, individuality, and neurosis. There is no choice. As the legend has it,[14] we are brought into this world against our will and we are taken from it—just about the time the wisdom that can only come with white hair lets us finally understand the mystery of generations—also against our will.

The path on which Abraham is lead by this "runaway" calf leads off into a field. Down into a cave. To parents. Mother and Father. Eve and Adam come before light and Eden and great awareness. In this respect, psychotherapy and religious search also agree. Return to parents must come early on in the journey. Not for gratitude—guilt (that they gave us life); or for anger—hatred (that they made such a mess of it); but that we might freely ponder what they did and did not do for us and what we did and did not do to them. "The story of Eden is a greater allegory than man has ever guessed. For it was truly man who, walking memoryless through bars of sunlight and shade in the morning of the world, sat down and passed a wondering hand across his heavy forehead. Time and darkness, knowledge of good and evil, have walked with him ever since."[15]

I have learned this story twice in my own lifetime. Once, when it happened to me, I did not know it was a story. But when I watched (what I imagined to be) the same story happening to my youngest son, and because I watched, I was able to understand that it was a story.

After the leaves have fallen there is nothing left through which to diffuse the sunlight. It cracks November cold through the window over the sink and is scattered like playing cards all over the kitchen floor. The two-year-old is alone with his mother and unaware that I am quietly watching from the doorway. My wife is standing at the sink. And the little boy is puttering on the floor nearby. How wonderful to have mother all to himself. And I am trying to remember our kitchen floor back on Collingwood Avenue. Where I am sure I once did what he is doing. What must it feel like for children whose holy memories are just now being formed? Those halcyon mornings seem so long ago. More distant than lifetimes. As far away in time as Adam and Eve. Each individual reenacts the history of humanity. Ontogeny recapitulating phylogeny. Why is what is forgotten forgotten? And why is what is remembered remembered?

Why can't we have it all the time? Why must there be spaces between the words and the letters? Why could it not be that all the letters of the Torah comprise one name of God? One totality, which to our pre-messianic eyes appears as separate letters. Why was the light by which the world was created hidden away? Why do we forget the location of childhood's garden? Or the course of the river of light? Freud's answer is that, as children, we once intended to do something so terrible that for culture's survival it had to be repressed. It is better to forget about incest, murder, and cannibalism; our subconscious is, perhaps, everything forgotten. Such are the discontents of civilization and the universal human neurosis.[16] Others, like Huston Smith, have suggested that our amnesia is caused by a foolish over-reliance on scientific materialism.[17] And Julian Jaynes suggests that it comes on account of the breakdown of the bicameral mind. Where once we "heard" one-half of our brain speaking to the other, now there is consciousness and unconsciousness.[18] But about one thing all the traditions seem to agree. Where once there was light and truth and remembering and uninterrupted intercourse with the gods, now there are only fragments, dream, and forgetfulness. There once was light. Now it has been forgotten. Once we knew more than we can now remember. Religion and myth and therapy and dream are very much alike, and all are potentially valid ways of remembering. Returning. Regaining access to the river of light.

Perhaps the answer to our amnesia is already in the Eden story. Not in the simple moralism of disobedience and punishment, but even more apparent than that. It is not that what we saw/heard/tasted had to be repressed, or that we are too scientific, or that our minds are now split, or even that what we knew has been outgrown and for good reason forgotten. It is not that the first human beings were sinful, or that all their children were sinful on account of them, or because of their own penchants for acting as they did. Of course, all of those things are probably accurate. But there is an answer that has been around a very long time, and comes from everyone's grandparents. It is right there in the story: we have forgotten the eternal life of the Garden because we chose to. We freely traded it for a lifetime in this world. We gladly exchanged eternal life for a measly span of four score years and ten. Eternity for the twinkling of an eye. Everything for one afternoon of individuality. Here is the story:

"When a man and a woman conceive . . . God gestures to the angel appointed over souls and says, 'Bring me a particular soul, whose name is so and so and whose description is such and such who is [now] in the Garden of Eden. . . . Immediately the angel brings the soul before the Holy One (blessed is His Name). . . . A Light is lit over its head (Job 29:2–3) . . . and it beholds and gazes from one end of eternity to the other . . . from morning into evening . . . everything. When its time comes to go out into the air of the world, the light is extinguished . . . the infant forgets everything which it has seen. . . ."[19]

In its more universal version, we learn of *Adam Kadmon,* the primordial human being (sometimes the same as *Adam HaRishon,* the first human being): "That all the people of all generations stood before Adam, in the form in which they would enter the world, the souls of all of them were traced out before him in the firmament in the image of their shape in this world. . . ."[20] All the generations destined to come forth from him, standing and rejoicing before him."[21]

And in its most popular form, it goes like this. "The Lord God planted a garden in Eden, in the East, and placed there the man whom He had formed . . . with the tree of life in the middle of the garden (Gen. 2:8–9). . . . And the Lord God commanded the man saying, 'Of every tree of the garden you are free to eat; but as for the tree . . . you must not eat of it, for as soon as you eat of it you shall die" (Gen. 2:15–17).

Notice that at the beginning of the Eden dream there is only one tree. In the middle of the Garden. Everything grows from it. All the other roots and branches and leaves drawing life from the earth and offering it back toward the heavens are only imperfect replicas of the one in the center: the tree of life. And that is probably all there originally was. None of this good and evil business. No moralizing. No temptation. No guilt. At the center of paradise there is life. And the paradox: if you eat of its fruit you will die. You will have to work to stay alive and bring forth your babies with labor. No more childhood. At this level of the story, the tree of life is also ultimate knowledge. Life precedes knowledge. It is only later, as subsequent generations seek to justify human discomfort as being on account of sin, that our ineluctable urge to know about life becomes disobedience and the tree of life is split in two: the tree of the knowledge of good and evil, and the tree of life. Who would tell of a garden with two trees at the center? There was and is only one tree at one center, and every human being tastes of its fruit.

"So the Lord God banished him from the Garden of Eden . . . and stationed east of the Garden of Eden the cherubim and the fiery ever-turning sword, to guard the way to the tree of life" (Gen. 3:23–4). It is back to this embryonic garden that Abraham follows the calf. Back down through mother earth's womb. Past the figures of Adam and Eve. After the light that was once extinguished. Back to Eden.

There was a time when the first person and every person beheld everything in the primordial light of consciousness. Saw from one end of being into the other. This time preceded birth, or at least sexual maturity. Its light is now gone. We have been expelled from seeing what our eyes once saw. Where once there was knowing everything, now there are only the scattered pieces of memory. An occasional déjà vu. A random dream. And of course the myths themselves.

## CHILDREN OF THE GARDEN

If you would grow up, you must leave the garden. And once you leave the garden you must die. Only in sexuality is the great paradox endured. Both forbidden knowledge consumed and immortality through procreation insured. "And they *knew* they were naked . . ." (Gen. 3:7).

As theologian Richard Rubenstein observed, "Sexuality is humanity's necessary response to the mortality with which Adam is cursed as a result of his offense. Without death men would have no need to procreate. The author of the biblical story intuits the connection between sex and death. Sexuality is not Adam's sin. It follows from his punishment."[22]

To become a person is to choose to "learn" the secret of life, which your parents had to know in order to conceive you and have forbidden you to learn. "You may eat from every tree in the Garden except for the one that will enable you to be like one of us." (Let us make someone in our image.) So the Eden story is at least the drama of an adolescent learning of procreation and accepting, as a consequence of his or her disobedience, being sent out of the house. (In America, in order to control the labor pool, the setting out and making one's own garden is often postponed until graduate school; but the banishment—even though it takes a decade—is nevertheless commenced.) Being content to remain a child is to concede the secret of life to your parents.

The act of primal promethean disobedience, by this interpretation, is reenacted by every human being, as it must be. For each one of us says I must find out the secret, even if it means I shall someday die ("and the two of them saw that they were naked" [Gen. 3:7]). Mother, Father—this means you, too—one day choose

44

to learn the secret. And that you will die. And that I am born so that you can live forever. And that through you I am really Adam and Eve's child.

To each soul is given the permission to choose between remaining in the Garden, eating from every tree except one, having not a care in the world. Seeing and knowing everything. Polymorphously perverse. Allowing God to be parent. Remaining a child all one's days and therefore remaining also childless. And therefore freezing childhood and living forever, or: eating from the tree. Being disobediently human. Expulsion from the Garden. Estrangement from parent/God. Repression. Neurosis. Sin. Death. Growing up. Procreation. Parenthood. Sexuality, forgetting (which means learning for ourselves), and what we here know as real life. That is: entering the chain of the generations.

It has always impressed me as ironic that the Torah scroll of the Five Books of Moses, the central document of God's revelation for humanity in Judaism, should also be called a tree of life. From which we were forbidden to eat. From which we eat. It is at once the means of our fall and the means of our entering the chain of the generations.

Ultimately, all we seek to learn is what we as children once knew in the Garden. But forgot in order that we might live as real people; that the child in us might never be stilled. "This reawakening to childhood constitutes the goal of the psychotherapeutic process. The lifting of the childhood amnesia . . . has as its aim the reorganization of experience into essentially childlike human terms. . . ."[23] Not childishness . . . but childlikeness characterized by activity and reflected in attentive involvement, openness to experience, readiness for surprise, willingness to stand uncertainty, and the capacity to shift flexibly the focus of perception and inquiry."[24] That is what it was like in Eden.

Human beings remain children longer than any other creatures. Despite all our technology, it still takes a good thirteen years to attain full physiological maturity. A fact that is certainly near the center if not the very cause of human culture. Because infants are so helpless, there must be some ongoing organization to protect and nurture them until they are old enough to perpetuate the species. Some students, upon noticing the striking similarity between ape and human infants,[25] have suggested that—were it not for the comparatively large size of the human head at birth—we might have been better off remaining *in utero* until we were older.[26] Perhaps even until we were fully mature? Just how such a situation would affect culture is, of course, preposterous to imagine; but it would certainly rearrange the oedipal drama. We have to be born early, before it is time. The choice is between heads too big to pass through a mother's pelvis and thirteen years of sexual immaturity, or being born fully grown and wisened, but killing the one who bears us. Again, it comes down to life or knowledge. In any case, our time in the "garden" begins with conception and extends for nine months and thirteen years, until we are able ourselves to procreate. Birth is but one of a legion of childhood traumas and perhaps not even the first one at that.

And so it is that as the years come upon us we gain a greater reverence for the flow of the generations. Our seeming wisdom only adds to the mystery of those who have come before and without whom we would not be, and through whom we seem to receive little pieces of some great image of being. We are increasingly impressed with the inherited knowledge of our ancestors. More reverent toward their heirlooms. Able now to listen to the legends with greater concentration. "Inquire of generations gone by, they will tell you; ask your parents, they will inform you" (Deut. 32:7).

It is very easy. As simple as a father speaking to his son just after the boy has read from the Torah to become a Bar Mitzvah. He says, we love you and we are proud of you. You are our hope and our seed for the future. And then he says to his grown-up little boy, I remember how your grandfather, my father, was there when you were born. And how he prayed he would live to see this day when you would read from the Torah. (But the old man is absent. Died many years ago. God, how he wanted to be here.) I am sorry, my son. Now it is only you and I. The chain goes on. May I live to be present when your children read from the Torah. And if it is not meant to be for me either, then please will you say something like this for me. Everyone cries. Drops of water, you know, are a universal symbol for resurrection of the dead.

By the time you're old enough to do what you've been waiting to be old enough to do, it has all changed into a world that you did not make or want. And in trying to make what is into what was, you succeed only in making it into something yet to be, which your children won't want either.

But at least you can tell them the stories. These will link them back to a time in humanity's *intra uterine* childhood when everything was of one totality. When there was no amnesia. Abraham, I imagine, looks at Adam (his father), realizes he is not dying, and asks, "Why is it taught that I cannot see you until I am about to die?" Whereupon Abraham's consciousness completes the circle of self-reflection. This near-death of self-awareness, according to Western spiritual tradition, also happened to an entire people.

# Chapter 3

# The Self-Reflection at Sinai

*What then enters into consciousness is an awareness of one's world image precisely as an image of reality and not reality itself. Instead there is reason to assume that the so called mystical experience occurs when for whatever momentary reason we manage to leave the curved space of the self-reflectiveness of our own world image and for a fleeting moment succeed in seeing it from the outside . . . this is not a terrifying moment of disintegration and dissolution of reality but rather conveys a sense of liberation and of ultimate existential security.*

*—Paul Watzlawick[1]*

*The* Sod *(Secret) of the* Torah *does not refer to the* Kabbala *(esoteric mystical tradition). For those things are already found in revealed texts, and since anyone who desires may learn them and study them with a* Haver *(learning partner) we can hardly call them secret. So the real meaning of "secret" with regard to the* Torah, *must refer to what is revealed to everyone according to their particular degree of spiritual advancement in the Torah. And this indeed is the meaning of "secret" and not something which (any)one is able to learn with his friend or his student; but that which remains for each individual according to their own unique abilities and rung.*

*—Rabbi Kalynomos Kalmish*
*(Shapiro) of Pieasetsna[2]*

*If* you look at Adam you will die. All the sources agree. Yet Abraham saw him and even spoke with him and was spared. There, at that moment of seeing what in waking consciousness cannot be seen, the journey toward consciousness has its real beginning.

There were others before and surely there will be others (including ourselves) after Abraham who have tried to enter the cave, to "behold one's parents." Some are punished. Some are driven mad. And some merely give up. But all of them and all of us share this peculiar human gnawing to comprehend our own being. To somehow (re)experience our conception(s). To see the whole picture without removing ourselves from it. To be at once the subject and the object. Notice how these words and phrases have multiple meanings. Is it perhaps that, as we return closer to the origin of our own consciousness, the metaphors themselves crack and buckle?

In the metaphor of this story, Abraham—the first one to realize that there is a Holy One to all Being—is now about to look in the mirror. In standing before Adam, Abraham—partly due to his own zeal, but mainly due to some act of grace (he does not die, even though his ego might endure something like its own death)—comprehends not only his own parents but, symbolically, his own consciousness. The wide-eyed unself-aware consciousness of the dawn-man now raises itself above the ocean and tries to become aware of itself in the very moment *of its own awareness—without dying. "Man had escaped out of the eternal present of the animal world into a knowledge of past and future. . . . The Eden . . . that the animal world had known for ages was shattered at last. Through the human mind, time and darkness, good and evil, would enter and possess the world.[3] Lacking a language capable of shuttling between ordinary awareness and awareness that is capable of self-reflection, myth and dream often speak of it as death. Certainly anyone who could endure "meeting Adam" and "live" to tell about it, would be changed. Abraham, says our story, does look up and see the light emanating from Eden itself!*

*This self-reflection of consciousness is the touchstone for all religions. Our consciousness, for a moment, inverts itself and we yet live on. In Judaism this moment is Sinai. An entire people lives through one moment when the first letter, which has no sound, was heard. And it seems that likewise, in Christianity, there was this moment when the Holy One of Being took the form of a person. A son was given. Father and son beheld one another and Christians, through their faith in the Christ, may reenter this timeless moment as well. The Torah was, you will recall, deliberately given in a land that belonged to no one.*

## THE SELF-REFLECTION OF CONSCIOUSNESS

Sinai is the story of a time when, for just a moment, we became aware of our own awareness. Self-conscious of our own consciousness. The light of the first verses of Genesis is a metaphor for the dawning of human awareness.[4] In one sense, all of Scripture is the story of the discovery of and straying from that light. But, until Sinai, the light was unaware of itself: a child who did not know it could see. Not until the mountain did we become conscious of the medium by which we are conscious. Vision was turned back into itself, creating the momentary sensation of blindness. The light must have been too bright, for we said, "Let not God speak to us, lest we die" (Exod. 20:16).[5]

And later, even the One of Being confides in Moses, the translator, that "a human being shall not see my face and live" (Exod. 33:20). Awareness may not behold itself while it is in the act of beholding itself. Could a fish learn of how fishes swim in water by watching them from dry land—unless, of course, it was in the few twitching moments before its death? Like the student of Zen who tried to ask the ultimate existential question, "Who am I?" only to be surprised by the voice that replied, "Who is it who is asking?" Could we, as Franz Rosenzweig asked, take out our eyes to see how we see? No. Immediacy may not reflect upon immediacy and remain both itself and in the present.

"You shall not see my face and live." If you are willing to die, then perhaps we can do business. But as long as you hang on to your ego, your selfhood, going around being a subject, comprehending other subjects and thereby making them objects, you will not see me.

Here might lie the meaning of God's strange reply to Moses: "After I pass, I shall remove my hand and you can see my back" (Exod. 33:23). On a literal, anthropomorphic level, it is obviously nonsense; but if we consider it as Moses' discovery that immediacy cannot be self-reflective, that consciousness cannot turn back upon itself, then a new understanding emerges. Especially if we remember that the Hebrew word *acher,* back, also has a temporal sense. "The best you can hope for," God tells Moses, "is to see what it is like just after I have been there." Is this not the fate of any religious person—to perpetually stand awestruck? Contemplating the One who can only be met in the present but comprehended in the past tense. We cannot know God in the future. And, as we have seen, immediacy is out of the question. But, "When I remove my hand, you will be able to see my back."

This Sinai story, of how we once endured the self-reflection of our own consciousness, tells that there are not one, but two parts:

two becomings conscious. You will recall that there were two sets of commandments. The first set were either withdrawn or smashed. According to one legend, when God gave the commandments, everyone died.[6] The One of Being apparently did not yet know that human beings could not look upon Being face to face and live. Humanity unable to survive infinity. So God, in a retrospective act of grace, took the commandments back. And everyone came back to life. According to the other, more popular version, the bargain was shattered in an act of Mosaic rage over the business with the calf. But, in either case, the first attempt on the part of the Holy One to covenant with Israel failed. In other words, the first try at fathoming our own awareness fails. There is some dying or shattering in between. And then, the second set is given and received without much fuss at all. Which leads us to suspect that, since death and brokenness are still so frequent, the second giving (coming?) has not happened. That the second set has not yet been given and that all we possess are the broken fragments of the first set, which were nevertheless also carried in the ark.[7] Imagine it: a sacred chest filled with shattered words and pieces of stone. We live in a time after the confusion of trying to endure the self-reflection of our own consciousness, but before we have succeeded.

Mirrors at the time of death. Culture's greatest creation for pondering the mystery of self-reference is, of course, the mirror. And it is just this invention found everywhere in the world that —according to Jewish folk tradition, on the occasion of death— must be covered up. Is it not perhaps a way of saying that the ultimate outcome of self-reflection is death? Or perhaps even a way of saying that, when the frail gauze separating this world of life and the other world of death has been momentarily torn, we must be especially careful to keep the portal of the mirror closed, lest there be additional passages going this way and that, between life and death. Let us instead cover the mirrors, doing the best we can to endure the mystery and pain.

One might tell a story of how it was that we first became aware that we were aware. The one about Sinai again, but this time without asking ourselves to imagine the One of Being anthropomorphically. And without even asking one another to believe God spoke in words or wrote with a finger. It would remain a very compelling and awesome recounting: once this man, whom we call Moses, went up on Sinai. Tending God's flock. And there he had an experience of fire that should have consumed but did not. He "heard" the "voice" of the One of Being speaking to him from out of the bush. And the One of Being said only and all that the One of Being ever says, "I am." I will be who I will be; I am who I am; I am the One of Being; I am the Lord your God. (It is all the same.) When you become aware you are aware, you will know who I am, even as when you learn who I am, you will become aware of who you are. With that, Moses' hair turned white (acquired wisdom? grew up? scared to death?). And he went and lead all "slaves," who wished to at last be free, back to that unconsumable thorn bush, where the One of Being said again— and this time to all of them—"I am." But they said, "Let not God speak to us lest we die." And in this way a dim but unmistakable awareness of consciousness entered the world.

The bush in its pristine loneliness is a prototype and a prophecy of the mountain yet to come. There are some things one sees that, like the bush, "consume" all of a person and demand only that he soon return, bringing as many others as he can along with him. The great paradigm within the Western myth of self-awareness is the public spectacle of a few years later at Sinai; even as Elijah's own lonely hearing of the "still small voice" is an echo or a memory of that same Sinai event generations later. It keeps happening. The bush and the slaves and Moses and Elijah are all present within one another and you and me. Some scholars have even suggested that, at the historical time of the going out from Egypt, the idea of individuated selves that we know today did not exist. There was only the corporate body of the people. Their experience of revelation was as a whole people. God may have "spoken" to one organism! In which case it may have been, as it is today, one against one. This one against the One.

Each age must in its turn recall this memory of how we have sought to become aware of our own consciousness, and understand it for itself. For each age looks back on the event and sees a different problem. For us, the question is not so much one of whether or not Spirit speaks, but from whence comes its voice.


## THE SOURCE OF THE VOICE

Within the Western religions of revelation, everything depends on the source of the Voice. If it comes from beyond people, then there is a God. If it comes from within them, then there is not. And if you do not understand that word, then we can substitute phrases like "source of meaning," "ground of being", or "ultimate awareness." It matters little how we describe this god, or how or to whom this god speaks.

The orthodox claim "He" spoke once and for all at Sinai—but that we were all there to hear it. The point is that God is more than us, other than us. Different from us. Beyond us. And, especially, outside us. If humanity ceased to be, the voice would still sound though no one would be there to hear. In either case, with or without people to listen, the documents of revelation can at least in principle be records of God's truth. This is the key point: the Holy One is more than us. And since God's voice issues from the outside, it instructs, chastens, and commands. Since the voice is exclusively from outside, God is wholly other than us.

If on the other hand, as liberals claim, the voice comes from within, then the spiritual enterprise is inverted. Religion is inescapably humanism. It makes little difference here whether the voice from within is heard as (divine) inspiration, conscience, insight, or intuition. What matters is that if all people were to vanish from the earth, the voice would surely disappear with them. Since the voice is exclusively from the inside, there is no God but humanity.

There are, of course, more complicated versions of these two choices. God might, in fact, be beyond us but only speak through us. Or, conversely, God might only be a human invention whose voice is projected outwards and then reflected back from the heavens. But, in either case, the final question remains: what is the real source of the voice?

We might accuse the theists ("God's voice only comes from without") of being afraid to trust themselves; or the humanists ("God's voice is only human") of mistrusting the very universe that bore them. Each psychological/theological position goes on to accuse anyone who "hears" voices from the "other" direction of being blasphemous or simply stupid. ("How dare you attribute God's words to human invention!?" "Only people speak; all else is poetry, and to take poetry literally is to pervert it!")

But the duality goes beyond this. Our psyches and our culture are also split along this axis of without and within. We seem to need the outside to make something real and the inside to make it worthwhile. One of the distinctive features of the Western psyche is its ruthless division of the universe into exterior and interior. Public and private. Objective and subjective. Matter and mind. Sciences and humanities. What is outside the body is thing. It is not-I. It is quantifiable and through the very process of quantification is kept at a safe distance. Since it is unlike me, it can be used. It is cold and lifeless and can make no personal or moral claim on my being. It is the world of the I-it. And, in truth, this is one of our goals: to render everything a thing. And thereby control it. To take even what is physically within our bodies and put it outside. (Fascination with increasingly abstract forms of quantification and varieties of spirituality are often disguised forms of such anality.[8]) What is inside the body is person. It is I. It has feelings. It may be warm and even, at times, confusing, but it is life. But it is what is outside the Western body that counts. That is where the real world is. Again, it is obvious that there are many complicated versions of the great division—ones in which people piously or pathologically confuse the two worlds. There are souls who treat their beings as if they were lifeless, or who treat the universe as if it were alive. But for most of us, nurtured in the West, there does not seem to be a third alternative.

We may now understand the real stakes in whether the voice issues from without or within. And, above all, why it is so crucial to the very nature of our psyches themselves that there be this dichotomy. If the voice comes from without, then there is life outside us; there is reality outside us. If our whole way of encountering the world is radically split along the axis of objective and subjective, then it is hardly surprising that our culture's discussion of the source of life's ultimate meaning would be likewise divided. And this brings us again to Sinai and its array of myths. Here too the legends betray our continuing confusion over the source of the voice.

The Holy One of Being speaks, as it were, in two modes. There is the one whose voice comes from without and is thus named *HaShamayim,* the Heavens. This is a public, objective, commanding word, which informs so much of contemporary orthodox religion. Commenting on the verse "And all the people perceived all the thunderings" (Exod. 20:5), Rabbi Akiva said, "They saw a word of fire issuing from the mouth of the Almighty and hewn out upon the tablets."[9] From this voice, *MiPi HaShemua* ("from the mouth which is heard," says one tradition), came the last eight utterances (or commandments). Everyone present heard them. Even those who were not there. The voice went forth in all seventy known languages and in all directions at once.[10]

On the other hand, there is a mode of hearing the One of Being that is present in this place. This is the one whose Name is *Makom,* place. A personal, quiet—perhaps even feminine—and internal sound. The One who is here. Whose voice is a *bat kol,* the little girl of the voice. A God who spoke at Sinai with each individual intimately in the voice of his or her parents, according to his or her respective levels of strength and understanding. So as not to frighten them.[11] The very same voice that Moses heard in Midian saying, "Return to Egypt," Aaron, his brother, heard in Egypt saying, "Go into the wilderness to meet Moses."[12] Or, as the *Zohar* teaches, a voice that divides itself into six hundred thousand personal meanings appropriate to each soul there present.[13] This voice is the one that uttered the first two commandments (which some Christian traditions call the first one): "I am the Lord" (not itself even a commandment) and "You shall have no other gods besides Me." This voice was *MiPi HaGevurah,* "from the mouth of strength."[14] A voice that, according to a tale Scholem attributes to Rabbi Mendel Torum of Rymanov, was further limited to the first word and then to the very first almost soundless letter of the first word, *Aleph.* It is a letter that "represents nothing more than the position taken by the larynx when a word begins with a vowel. Thus the *Aleph* may be said to denote the source of all articulate sound . . . [and] to hear the Aleph is to hear nothing."[15]

Philosopher Emil Fackenheim once wisely suggested that, if an agnostic had been present at Mount Sinai, he would have heard the thunder and seen the lightning but wondered what all the commotion was about. To which we might add that, had we been there, we would have doubtless been paralyzed by our inability to decide whether the voice came from outside or inside ourselves—when, of course, it is clear now that the choice itself is spurious. For the voice, if it be truly the voice of the Holy One of Being, speaks from both without and within. And it is the same voice.

" 'How then is it possible to know God in *all* ways?' asked Rabbi Pinḥas of Koretz. 'It is because when God gave the Torah, the whole world was filled with the Torah. Thus there is nothing that did not contain Torah, and this is the meaning of the verse. Whoever says that the Torah is one thing and the profane sphere is another is a heretic.' "[16]

## THE TORAH OF MOSES AND
## THE TORAH OF ELIJAH

The Midrash teaches that Moses and Elijah are the same man.[17] And indeed, after some reflection, we discover that the situations of their lives are remarkably similar. Both men at one time seem to be the only person remaining in all of Israel who remembers the living God. The people have gone over to the calf. They have taken up with Baal. And they each called for a showdown between the Lord of the universe and a dead idol of self-destruction. And both went up alone on the mountain of Horeb-Sinai for forty days and forty nights. And each one of them was, for his own protection, hidden by God in some since-before-the-world-was-created cleft cave in the rock.[18] And there they received the word. Saw the light. Heard the voice. In other words: they are of the same archetype.[19] Or, in still other words, the holy myth of receiving the Torah has not one but at least two heroes. Two versions of the God/person encounter at Sinai.

Strikingly similar. And they correspond, not surprisingly, to the two sources of the voice.

We already know well the Moses version of the one who hears the voice. It is the dominant mode of Western revealed religion. The Elijah side, however, is far less accessible to our customary ways of religious learning. (Even though, to be sure, we often tell of Elijah as if he were like a Moses, in the same way we are blind to that dimension of Moses that is Elijah.) Elijah too has his own special relationship to the One of Being. He performs big miracles, works with ecstatic zeal, and literally goes out in a blaze of glory. And Elijah was crazy. Because of his zeal and doubtless his charisma, in Judaism he is the "messenger of God" par excellence. Appearing almost ubiquitously. Invisibly. At every Passover seder (during whose traditional liturgy the name of Moses is virtually ignored) a place is set for this wanderer. This consorter with children. This itinerant teacher who will be the first to bring us the good tidings of the Messiah. Consider *his* version of the climb up the mountain of Sinai: After winning the final showdown with the priests of Baal, but ensuring his future as an enemy of Jezebel, the queen, he is forced to flee to the wilderness. Alone. No mixed multitude following. No six hundred thousand freed slaves. No Charlton Heston, no seven-foot-tall white-bearded hero. Elijah is alone in the cave. "I alone am left" (1 Kings 19:10).

And then the One of Being passed by. "And as my Presence passes by I will put you in a cleft of the rock . . ." (Exod. 33:22). "And there was a great wind—tearing mountains and shattering rocks." Now surely God would be present in such an event. "But God was not in the wind" (1 Kings 19:11). "After the wind an earthquake." But God was not there either. "And then a firestorm" (1 Kings 19:12). But God was not even in the firestorm. Here were all the sorts of events God had customarily chosen as vehicles of God's presence. Remember the Moses version: "Now Mount Sinai was all in smoke for the Lord had come down upon it in fire. . . . The whole mountain trembled violently. The blare of the horn grew louder and louder" (Exod. 19:18–19). Here are suitable theatrics for a public spectacle. It is almost as if the One of Being is saying to Elijah that God can and does appear this way, but not always, and that there is a side of being (an Elijah dimension to Moses) that does not and cannot discern the Holy voice in such mass, external, objective, public media as wind and fire. No, indeed. This God of Elijah, as we read in the next verse, speaks in a thin, barely audible, innermost voice. A *Kol D'mama Daka* (1 Kings 19:12).

Rabbinic tradition is not in agreement with exactly what such a sound is, or even what its "barely audibleness" teaches. There is, at least, consistency in the fact that this voice of God is very quiet and could be heard only by one who was even quieter. As Rashi says, "And I have heard that the voice comes from the midst of silence. . . ." In the words of the *Zohar,* this sound originates from "the very innermost point which is the source of all illumination."[20] Therefore, it has always seemed to me that the *Kol D'mama Daka* is the sound we make as breath is exhaled through our lips. (Go ahead. Listen to the barely audible sound of breath leaving your lungs and flowing out through your mouth.) It produces, if you will, a kind of no-sound, like Rabbi Mendel Torum of Rymakov's tale of Moses' earlier encounter with God on that same mountain place, which also had the no-sound of the first commandment's first letter of being, *Aleph.* And this, I believe, is the internal innermost private side of the ineffable voice of being.

So while there may have been but one Sinai, there were at least two who were present: Moses and Elijah. Through Moses all the people. To them the voice came from outside. It was public, external, and objective. Their experience of the "I am the One of Being" has set, or been set by, the dominant mode of Western culture until this day. This is most of what most people today think of as Western revealed religion. It is the doctrine of Akiva, The Torah of Moses.

But there is another recollection of this event. Hidden, but transmitted through the Elijah legend. A foggy memory of one who heard the "I am the One of Being" as a barely audible internal breathing-like voice. A private, internal, and subjective memory, but nevertheless an equally abiding wonder. Indeed, the mystics have an ancient tradition of "validating" their "personal revelations" as *gilluiy Eliyahu,* revelations of Elijah. Or, as Gershom Scholem, teacher of the "new gnosis," has taught, "On the threshold of mystical revelation [the Jewish mystic] encounters the prophet Elijah. . . ."[21] This other internal voice is the Torah of Elijah. And this then, is the point: there are two Torahs. Not, as according to the orthodox Jewish myth, a written and an oral one, but an external and an internal one. Both are indispensable to a living spiritual tradition even as we must constantly remember that both—Moses and Elijah—are the same person. And this, then, is the second point: the Torah of Moses is the same as the Torah of Elijah.

The One of Being did not speak from without *or* from within, but from without *and* from within. The inevitable conclusion of balancing the Torah of Moses with the Torah of Elijah is not to diminish one or elevate the other. Not to give it all away to self-fearing, guilt-ridden fundamentalists or to self-serving, anarchist, premature messianists. Our goal must be to restore the balance, to place the source of the voice, the source of reality, *everywhere.* Inside us *and* outside us. The "I am the One of Being," which one tradition heard from on top of the mountain, could also have been heard from within each person.

Even as we say this we fear we shall be accused of heresy (a charge not unbecoming a movement for spiritual renewal). Defenders of the faith will insist that if God speaks also from within, then we have done away with piety's commanding, external, objective, public dimension. Now everyone will surely go about doing what is good in his or her own eyes—to the utter ruin of all. Whereupon we must remind tradition's defenders and ourselves that the voice within is the *same* as the voice without. They are not different voices. Moses and Elijah are the same person.

But surely to join inner and outer voices is to invite false prophets, ordinary liars, and schizophrenics into our midst. After all, both crazy people and liars, for their own reasons, cannot or will not distinguish between their own inner voices and ones that "really" come from without. The borders of their selves are blurred. For our part, we who hope we are not crazy and believe we are not lying (nervous assertions both) frequently label others crazy or deceitful who threaten our own agreed-upon reality. The only tests we finally have are the majority's reasoned opinion over the years and generations (was Jeremiah or Ezekiel or Sabbatai Zevi crazy?) and our own intuition. (Religiosity is often a hedge for madness, the most pious frequently standing closest to the borderline.) Often, society's reasoned opinion and our own intuition do not themselves coincide. These things must be judged as they arise. We must simply be willing to withstand charges of heresy—weighing them, too, in the light of their own motivations and our understanding that they are there specifically to keep things the way they are.

Let there be no confusion. The Torah of Elijah wrests the control of religion—and through it of morality and madness—from institutions entrusted with its perpetuation and preservation. But our goal has never been merely to perpetuate or preserve. We are not simply custodians of a tradition, not just keepers of a museum. Our goal is also to break it open. Set it free. Give to one another permission to hear and to speak the word. Whether old worn rehearsals of ancient public words or never-before-heard-even-by-us voices from that still, small, innermost self within. At first an awkward, halting melody. Unsure that the inner voice and the outer one will sound right together.

It is hardly an accident that the movement for spiritual renewal within contemporary liberal Judaism draws almost exclusively on mysticism and particularly on a Hasidism (filtered through Buber), which itself would return validation to the individual melodies of each soul. (We are reminded of Scholem's accusation that Buber was an anarchist.[22]) The simple truth is that individual, private, subjective religious melodies come together as a harmony with their ancient traditional counterparts. As Scholem teaches: "By assuming that the word of God is shining in many lights, reflected in infinite mirrors of meaning, the mystics could manage to read the old texts as speaking of their own innermost experience and vision. The rigid text that had become invested with the authority of revelation is . . . smelted down and recast in new forms."[23]

So it will come as no surprise that the "old texts" may on occasion crack and buckle and even shatter, spilling sparks of undreamed of light, which in turn seem to issue from our innermost soul. The Holy One does it to humanity with the word. Humanity reignites that holy word again and again with its piety, its insight, its intuition. It is easy; we are made of the same stuff as one another. In moments of heightened consciousness, cells of one being.

## THE LIMITS OF THE BODY

We must remind ourselves that when a man and a woman join in the act of procreation, one is literally inside the other. Is this not a part, perhaps, of its great mystery, fascination, and holiness? That the boundary between the universe and our innermost being is at last removed. More than just joining, outside and inside are open to one another. The Torah of Moses and the Torah of Elijah become one.

The farther away in space or time we look—or the closer we look—the more we are likely to be astonished to find empirical confirmation for our own intuition that *we are OF the cosmos and it is OF us.* The external universe, public, objective, Torah-of-Moses-empirical is not at all discrete from our so-called mind or our private, subjective, Torah-of-Elijah-innermost consciousness. They are of the same stuff. Their so-called borders are blurred and often simply erased. "The fluid in our bodies is a perfect replica of that ancient sea in which we grew to fruition following our liberation from the clay."[24]

Item: Every seven years all of the cells of our bodies (with the exception of the ova in women and some cells in our brains, which do exchange their molecular contents with their less permanent neighbors) die, are exhaled, excreted, cut off, fall, or are otherwise removed from us. We grow new skin surfaces each week, the blinking of our eyes flushes hundreds of cells down the tear ducts, and the entire linings of our mouths are washed away and digested with every meal.[25] To be replaced by new cells that will continue the specialized, sacred task of their "parents" before them. Until in their turn they too die. It does not happen all at once. The process is "organic" in the highest sense of that word. Part of life's sustaining rhythm. So we must understand that it is impossible to point to any part of our bodies and call it permanently ours, any more than we could own a breath of air. The ecosystem that sustains our life flows in, around, and through us. We literally exchange molecular contents with it with each breath. But more than that, we are literally made of it. Even as it is made of us.

Item: There are countless organisms that live within us, and without which we could not live. As Lewis Thomas says, "We are shared, rented, occupied."[26] We are more like walking, (sometimes) conscious ecosystems than discrete organisms. Little creatures within the cells of our bodies called mitochondria, by whose oxidated energy we live, the descendants of primitive bacteria who "probably swam into ancestral precursors of our eukaryotic cells and stayed there. Ever since, they have maintained themselves and their ways, replicating in their own fashion, privately, with their own DNA and RNA quite different from ours. . . . Without them we would not think a thought."[27]

Item: The physical borderlines of our "outer extremities," when viewed through the electron microscope, are much more like the coast of Maine than the clean, straight lines that appear to our naked eyes.

Item: There is high mathematical probability that some of the molecular stuff that has gone into, is in, or will go into what we conventionally call us, has come or will yet go to the furthest reaches of the cosmos. A breath of air. A cell on your eyelid, in a drop of sweat, or in the wall of your heart, has in all likelihood been to the edge of space!

Item: Such astonishment is temporal as well as spatial. There is an equally high mathematical probability that some of our molecular stuff has come from the primeval fireball of creation itself, the furnace in which the universe began. That we might literally have (for a while, at least) within our very bodies some of the matter that was there during the very first moment, or some of the air with which Moses reiterated what he had heard when he heard the One of Being say "I am"; or some of the air that carried that thin, barely audible sound of breathing, which calmed Elijah.

Notions of inside and outside may just be cultural convention. A once helpful, but now insidious trick persuading us to regard the locus of our consciousness within what we ordinarily call our bodies. Perhaps awareness is also outside us; independent of organic matter.[28] What if what we call "God" is intimately related to a mode of consciousness and our collective beings that we are not allowed or accustomed to call part of ourselves? For, in addition to being within us, it is also without us. Is this not the One who unites us all? The One who is beyond us, but whom we are forbidden to name as part of us? The One who is certainly our infinite potential, The Holy One of Being? We are made of the same quantum stuff as the rest of the cosmos. We are each, as it were, clones of the universe. A little bit of it has broken off inside and has developed its own transient "self-awareness." It is me. The cry of a newborn. Radio Station "It-is-I" now commences its regularly scheduled lifetime broadcast.

## THE REVELATION OF SILENCE

At the time of teaching, it is the teacher who—by some word or deed, a question, a blow, or simply through silence—forces the student to hear a voice that comes from within. All genuine learning is thus the self's disclosure to itself. The voice issues with such clarity that the ones who learn refuse to believe that it is their own. Insisting instead that it has come from the teacher who is across the room. All the great teachers share this alert passivity. A guide who is willing to draw out of the novice an innermost self, and who will remain long enough for a student to step back and discover what he or she has thought all along, or said, or done.

This student/teacher transaction is recreated by a therapist. Through transference, the patient comes to discover the archetypal relationships that have predetermined all relationships, have contaminated all conversations, sealed off each past word of address. The patient is able to hear what he or she has been saying all along. And in so doing the experience of insight is initiated.

How odd and yet how universal the misconception, on the part of all who would learn, that the knowledge they seek is outside them. To what lengths we go geographically, financially, and spiritually to find someone who will enable us to hear our own inner voice. And, of course, our culture's finest example of "the great learning" is what it calls theophany, the self-disclosure of God. At Sinai everyone is a student. According to our myth, all hear the voice of the Teacher. But not only is it a clear, publicly audible, external voice, it is also a voice that is the sound of our own breathing, a very precious, alert silence.

"And God spoke to each one at Sinai—so as not to frighten them —in the voice of their parents." So that is what my parents sounded like. I never really heard them until this time. And of course they must sound like their parents before them. All the way back to the first parents, who heard it from the animals, and the trees, who in turn heard it from the starry firmament overhead. Just this is the sound of the One of Being.

Suppose there were a voice that spoke something utterly new from utterly outside us, could we understand or even hear it? Is not all understanding dependent upon prior preparation and hope? The teacher must not go too fast. Insight must become as intuition. I cannot hear others screaming until I myself have learned to scream.

When Israel crossed the sea on dry ground (Exod. 14:22) it was the greatest show of the Holy One's saving power of all time. A common servant, at that hour, the Midrash teaches, beheld more than all the prophets![29] Yet, even there, those who saw did not behold. "The sea floor was covered, as one would expect, with mud, still moist from the ocean water. Whereupon one 'Reuben' remarked to one 'Simeon,' 'What's the difference?! In Egypt we had mud. Here we have mud.' "[30] There can be no external proof without prior awareness.

Could the One of Being say something at Sinai to someone who was not ready to hear it? Someone in whom the corresponding interior voice was not already latent—ready to be born? Would an Egyptian, on hearing the Sinai revelation, have heard?

In commenting on the verse, "They saw the voices" (Exod. 20:15), the *Zohar* suggests[31] that "everyone actually saw according to their abilities, for there is a tradition that they stood in groups each one seeing as befitted them."[32]

This raises a disturbing possibility. Suppose there were a "revelation" going on at this moment. But none of us have attained the prior readiness. We make too much noise, having forgotten how to be still. Are not the holy words themselves lost forever into the air? A whole civilization could be like one individual. Unable to see or listen to the voice that speaks from out of the river of light.

Rabbi Nachman of Bratzlav taught that "when one finally is included within *'eyn sof'* (the ultimate Nothingness), his torah is the Torah of God Himself, and his prayer is the Prayer of God Himself. . . ."[33] Among the Hasidim, eastern European spiritual revivalists of the eighteenth and nineteenth centuries, the word "Torah" acquired meaning beyond simply the scroll of The Five Books of Moses or even beyond a symbol of God's revelation to humanity. It began also to refer to a master's teaching. Particularly the oral teaching delivered at the table during a holy meal. The rabbi would "say Torah." Or, by implication, it might also denote the subsequently written down (or still oral) anthologies of his teachings, as in the "Torah" of rabbi so and so. In principle, there were as many different "Torahs" as there were teachers. And while it is true that many (most) teachings began with a verse from Scripture—that is, God's Torah—it is clear that there was no certain agreement or unanimity of these variegated teachings. Each rebbe had his own central and unique teaching. His own Torah. In other words, the One of Being utters a word that initiates revelation, even as we create ourselves by giving utterance to our own.

And this is, if you will permit, my Torah: that our own frequent reachings into that river of light that nourishes our psyche is our Torah. What we think and joke and muse—when we really tell the truth—is our Torah. "Rabbi Dov Baer [of Mezritch] said, I shall teach you the best way to say Torah. You must cease to be aware of yourselves. You must be nothing but an ear which hears what the universe of the word is constantly saying within you. The moment you start hearing what you yourself are saying, you must stop."[34] Or, to paraphrase Rabbi Kalonymos Kalmish (Shapiro) of Pieasetsna, God not only hears our prayers, God says them also.[35]

God, then, is not so much a speaker from the outside or a whisper from within, but the One on account of whom we hear "I am. . . ." And the medium of that revelation is silence. Rabbi Abahu taught in the name of Rabbi Yohanan, that when God said, "I am," no creature uttered a sound. Even the sea did not move. There was a deafening silence throughout the world. Only then did the voice issue.[36] So it is with all teaching.

And we come again to the paradox of any sustained spiritual search. A voice that speaks from the highest heavens and a voice from the inner chambers of the self. How could this possibly be? How could God who is infinite speak with people who are finite and not destroy them both?[37] How could a bush burn and not be consumed? "Let not the Lord talk to us lest we die!" (Exod. 20:16). How could consciousness behold itself in the very moment of its consciousness? How can the eye behold itself? It is all the same. And sooner or later all religious traditions must confront the impossible logic. (Indeed, their solution to that problem will determine the form their religion will take.) That what was without shall merge with what was within. Here is the common idea that all varieties of religion share. It is a kind of primary human experience toward which both science and religion converge. The Bible's image for the resolution of all paradox is the coming of the Messiah. The final transformation of consciousness itself. The Baal Shem Tov taught, "The coming of the Messiah does not depend upon anything supernatural, but rather upon human growth and self-transformation. . . . The world will only be transformed . . . when people realize that the Messiah is not someone wholly other than themselves."[38]

The more we become aware, the more we realize that we are in everything and everything is in us. The One we call the Holy One, and the ones the Holy One calls us, are the same beings, seen from different sides. So it is only natural that the voice be heard to issue from different directions. The question is not "Who makes who real?" People making God or God making people—for both make each other come to be. Both are One. *Yehido shel Olam.* The Only One of the Universe.

And our refusal to realize this, our inability to make it real, may just be the reason that the "anointed One" tarries. Surely the word would then break forth from children and their grandparents. From hewers of wood to the most erudite sages. From the first person to the last person. From even you and me. Protoplasm and consciousness aware of their common source.

# Chapter 4

# Protoplasm of Consciousness

*Adam was by nature a purely spiritual figure, a "great soul"
whose very body was a spiritual substance, an etheral body,
or body of Light . . . a microcosm reflecting the life of all the
worlds . . . a "great soul" in which the entire soul substance
of mankind (is) . . . concentrated. . . .*

*—Gershom Scholem[1]*

*There is a sense . . . in which the body is not real; but the
body that is not real is the false body of the separate self, the
reality ego. That false body we must cast off in order to begin
the odyssey of consciousness in quest of its own true body.*

*—Norman O. Brown[2]*

*The analysis of the physical world, pursued to sufficient
depth, will lead back in some now-hidden way to man himself, to conscious mind, tied unexpectedly through the very
acts of observation and participation to partnership in the
foundation of the universe.*

*—John Archibald Wheeler[3]*

*A*nd so there they are, Adam and
Abraham. Together in the cave. The beginning and the end of the first twenty
generations of humanity. One midrashic tradition tells that, had not Abraham
come along and figured out about the One of Being, the Presence would have
vanished from creation. Leaving behind a dross empty of even the possibility of
consciousness.[4] The Adam whose incorrigible human hungering after tree-of-life
fruit initiated humanity now meets the Abraham whose simple spiritual insight
that there is a Holy One of (or to) Being saves humanity. But Abraham is still
a little nervous. Remember, the legend warns that we only see Adam just before
we die. So Abraham instinctively covers his eyes. "Abraham," says Adam, "do
not be afraid. There is nothing to see. Everything that I am is already in you.
There is nothing to know. Everything that I learned is already within your
memory. Just as I was once shown you, so do you now see me. We are, both of
us, my child, of the same organism!"

We all issue from One Being. One undifferentiated Being. The soul of all souls.
Yehido shel Olam, "the Only One of the Universe." The memory of this
primordial unity is recorded in the chromosomes that shape our bodies. It is
transmitted unconsciously and genetically, and for this reason it is observable
everywhere throughout the universe. Thus it is only natural for the legend to tell
of how, when we die, we shall catch a glimpse of this primordial Adam and how

75

*it was possible for this Adam to behold all the generations. Just as each tiny thing carries within it the potential description of the whole of which it is a part. The iris of the eye. Handwritten words. The double spiral coil of dioxyriboneuclic acid. Our descriptions of an ink blot. Or any random dream's fragment. Each tiny piece, to the eyes and ears of one well trained, tells all about the whole.*

*Everything is organically connected to everything else in such a way that nothing is irretrievably and only a thing. Everything is part of a single organism. And each part "remembers" how once it, too, was part of a great unity that had no parts. And this primordial being is called, in Judaism,* **Adam Kadmon**, *a humanoid from whom the universe began.*

## CELLS OF ONE ORGANISM

If we go back far enough, through our common childhood, and our parents and their parents before them, sooner or later we come to the first parents. The first mother and father. And if we go back before that couple, we come to the first parent, the Adam of the first chapter of Genesis, who was androgynous.[5] One presexual organism. The first human being, *Adam Rishon.* He was very big. A giant. Maybe as big as the Garden, with its tree in the center and the four rivers flowing out from there. Maybe as big as the world. The parent of all nature. One great Adam, *Adam HaGadol.*[6] Rabbi Juda said that Rab said: Extending from one horizon to the other[7] and from earth to heaven.[8] A person of such beauty that the very sole of his foot obscured the splendor of the sun.[9] Containing the soul-sparks of all the generations yet to come.[10] It is as if Adam broke into the several billion individual pieces called humanity. And it is for this reason that the seers of old could look through a person's forehead, through all the forms that person's soul had traveled, all the way back to the great body of *Adam Rishon.*

Before this was a being bigger than the world. Larger and

brighter and perhaps containing even more than just organic seeds. One with proportions as enormous as the entire (expanding and contracting) universe. The Kabbalists called such a one *Adam Kadmon,* the primordial human being. Somewhere between the *Ayn Sof,* the One without end, and the first human. One in whom all creation occurs. The one whose psyche is the laws of nature and whose nerves are made of galaxies and lightning and of whom this third planet from the star we call our sun might be a single cell.[11] A kind of transition between the One without end and ourselves, whose years number three score and ten. An intermediary. A middleman. A real missing link between Creator and creature. A being of pure light,[12] whose form we imagine might occasionally be visible in the arrangement of stars on a clear country night. Or perhaps in the reflection of droplets of dew on flowers or in certain configurations of notes or molecules imagined under yet uninvented microscopes. An Adam who eclipses the horizons and the expanse of the heavens. Even before the creation. Before there was a before. *Adon Olam,* the Lord of Being. This one would be the Holy One of Being. The One who is *Ayn Sof,* the One who is beyond infinity. Beyond this is only the Self. The one who reads these words and for a moment understands. For a moment can almost remember. At this moment the circle closes on itself. It is a mystical body from which we are descended, in which we participate, and by whom we endure.[13] We are cells of one being.

According to some versions of the *Adam Kadmon* legend, we may each trace our ancestry back to specific "limbs" of that first human "tree." Some were branches, others trunk, and still others roots. All organically connected to one another. More than a common history, it is a biologic, a genetic connection. A single living being. It is for this reason that we even now feel a strange kinship with apparent strangers, for once we were literally next to one another. This might explain why, on some deep intuitive level, our psychospiritual modes are so similar. The "body" of humanity has an organic history like that of any individual. There was a moment when the potentiality for all the molecules was actually present in one cell. Just as in human embryonic development, one un-differentiated cell was filled with the promise of all creation. Furthermore, parts of any body may be unconscious; indeed, some are, like hair and nails, dead. But still they are parts. Each with its own sometimes indispensable function. Therefore let us not exclude animals and plants and even "dead" minerals from this body of *Adam Kadmon.* Each part was once the same as every other. But now, owing to its location in the "great body" of this lifetime, and, on account of its necessarily specialized function, those who were once twins, side by side in the same womb, are now unrecognizable as even similar. On account of where we have been, we are different.

And so it is also that, on account of where we are, we are different. This body of Adam, you see, has more than a historical sense. Now, at this moment, each one of the apparently disparate and hopelessly individuated parts is, in truth, part of one great organism. People whom we have never met and may never meet. Animals we cannot imagine. Plants as old as extinct monsters and too small to be seen even with microscopes. Glaciers and grains of sand and galaxies. Our own children. Mitochondria going about their business in our guts. Our own seeds. They are each but cells of the one great body that, due to our present spiritual limitations, cannot keep conscious of its spatial boundaries. It forgets that since everything is joined to every other thing, none can escape the pain or the joy of another. But such spatial awareness, like the temporal awareness of our own ancestral unity, requires such intense comprehension that we can only hold it within us for a moment. And then it is gone. We are powerless to hold it any longer. Unable even to reconstruct it.

There is, then, a literal sense in which we may speak of an enduring and present body of the primordial Adam, *Adam Kadmon.* Its universally common "protoplasm" is consciousness. The more consciousness, the more life, the more awareness. But from rocks to spirit, all being shares it. "The whole earth is filled with His glory" (Ps. 72:19). And this body of consciousness has a history that begins in a unicellular unity, and a present spatial reality that is also one living organism. And both images, historical and spatial, draw their respective unity from a consciousness that comprehends them. There is a consciousness that remembers all the evolutionary forms from the first being unto and up through the present multiplicity of forms that comprise the cosmos. And there is a consciousness that can comprehend all those present, apparently irreconcilable, individuals as if they were only facets of one living organism. (As on rare occasions some people can do with their own bodies.) And this consciousness within each and comprehending all is of course the same consciousness—even as it is within the eyes of the one who is reading these words.

All this is what I mean by the protoplasm of consciousness. And what I believe tradition meant by the primordial Adam and before that one, the *Yehido shel Olam.* The Only One of Being.

The universe is a "creation" in the highest sense of that word: something that has come forth from its Creator's uniqueness. Eternally bearing witness to its Creator. It is not some manufactured "thing," but an expression of being itself. The One of Being. *Yehido shel Olam,* the Only One of the Universe. One great breathing organism of which we are a part. Like a person, not a wristwatch. Even though it appears to us that most of its "parts" are unaware of their indispensable interrelatedness to all the other "parts," they are nevertheless more like the cells of one creature than they are like strewn pieces of some broken thing. "The earth's atmosphere is not simply a gaseous fluid into which substances are dumped by animals, plants, and factories, but the metabolism of a complex organism. . . ."[14] When viewed from space, our earth "has the organized, self-contained look of a live creature, full of information, marvelously skilled in handling the sun."[15] Just as we imagine that, viewed from a respectfully farther distance, this galaxy must also appear to be alive. Breathing in and breathing out. "Know that this universe, in its entirety is nothing else but one individual being . . . the variety of its substances . . . is like the variety of substances of a human being. . . ."[16] We are, along with animals and plants and mountains and stars, the cells of one being.

And as people are "of" the universe, the discreteness of one life from another is an illusion. A cultural convention of only limited survival value for our species. Upon closer observation, we fade into the background like a drop of dye in the ocean. Now we become aware of this "organism" that is our source and our destiny. "In the Unconscious . . . we are members of one another. . . . As long as we accept . . . the reality of the boundary between inside and outside, we do not 'really' incorporate each other."[17] The clear boundary lines of our bodies blur as we increase the microscopic magnification. We do not, when we are born, come into the world; we come out of it.[18] Myriads of cells each doing commerce with air and sound and water and light and countless yet-undiscovered other beings. Our bodily fluids are replicas of the primeval waters. And our substance is literally the stuff of mother earth. The electrical rhythms by which our "parts" work are the same in our heart of hearts and ten thousand miles overhead. "They" couldn't care less that they happen to run within and coincidentally sustain our bodies. We are, each one of us, mostly water (67 percent), water is two hydrogen atoms bonded to one oxygen atom. Each atom is itself 97 percent empty space.

"And God created man in His image, in the image of God He created Him; male and female He created them" (Gen. 1:27). We are more than "in the image" replicas. We are physically made of the very same stuff. Assembled in the same way. And according to the same blueprint. Not "similar" or "like" but "in the image of." Microcosms.[19] Fashioned by the same genetic code. So you see we are more like clones of God. And to study ourselves on the deepest level is to learn again of our Creator. Not someone who is other than us or beyond us but who somehow abides through all being.

This is precisely the gnostic heresy: that knowledge of the self —at the deepest level—is, simultaneously, knowledge of God.[20] The Baal Shem Tov once remarked to a disciple, "I explain that in this world, in the human being himself, all the mysteries exist. Thus I make a point out of raising matter to spirit."[21] That the Self and the divine are one and the same. In which case, psychotherapy is the legitimate heir (along with the new biology and the new physics) to the old gnostic traditions, since its promise is not even so much health and happiness, as it is self knowledge on the deepest levels. It offers only intuitive self-insight, which one may or may not choose to use. This primary gnostic equation of inner self and the Holy One is the touchstone for all spiritual renewal. One idea alone perpetually breaks away the accretions of centuries of piety: we are in the image. Surely this will be the Messiah's teaching.

Consciousness flows through all being and wants to realize itself through the human substance. The idea of Messiah is greater than the last human being or the ultimate human being. It is the ulti-

mate evolutionary form of consciousness. Through the person of
the Messiah we are returned again to our source. We are reunited
once again with all creation into one great common body of Adam.
This is an Adam who did not die: the ultimate body of consciousness. Look: some day it will happen in an unequivocal way. Something will happen to one person. It will be a great transformation.
The most hardened skeptic will have to confess that surely now
this person is as much spirit as matter. And once this happens
everyone will change. The great yearning will be realized. Once
again we will see our bodies mirrored in the heavens. For we will
see ourselves mirrored in the anointed one. *Adam Kadmon,* the first
one, will have become *Adam Aharon,* the last one. We too will be
no less than he/she is: in the image of God. And our transformation will change the ecosystem over which we have undisputed
charge. Then the spirit shall break forth from everywhere.

For Christianity, the central problem is how God could have
become person. How spirit could transform itself into matter.
Word become flesh. Consciousness become protoplasm. The direction is from the top down. For Judaism, on the other hand,
the problem is how humanity could possibly attain to God's
word and intention. How matter could raise itself to spirit. How
simple desert souls could hear the word. Human substance attain
consciousness. The intention is "to permeate matter and raise it
to spirit."[22] The direction is from the bottom up. Perhaps the
two traditions, one moving down, the other moving up, are destined to meet in the divinity of humanity. "R. Hoshaiah: When
the Holy One, blessed be He, created the first man, the minister-
ing angels mistook his identity and wished to say 'Holy' before
him. . . ."[23]

Human beings are joined to one another and to all creation.
Everything performing its intended task. Doing commerce with

its neighbors. Drawing nourishment and sustenance from unimagined other individuals. Coming into being, growing to maturity, procreating. Dying. Often without even the faintest awareness of its indispensable and vital function within the greater "body." None of our cells lives much longer than seven years. Only a few might endure from birth to death. And we larger collocations of cells called human beings, along with all the other creatures, and the stuff of the universe, are like the cells of one great living organism. Breathing in and out. Inhaling glaciers, exhaling cities. All creation is one person, one being, whose cells are connected to one another within a medium called consciousness. And when we rise to that medium, we sense the totality. We were not alive in the time of our great-great-grandparents. Nor can we visit every place in the cosmos. But sacred myth and legend bring what was ancient and what is distant right up before us this day. And thus, through the stories, we rise above the cultural convention that persuades us to regard the locus of our consciousness and our lives as being within what we ordinarily call our lifetime's body. The first human being, Adam, is the last human being, the anointed One, the Messiah. And we who are after the first "cell" but before the last are somehow within the only being that has ever been or will yet be. The *Yehido shel Olam*, the only One of Being. *Adam Kadmon*, the archetype of every person.

## GENETIC TRANSMISSION OF MEMORY

Holy stories we know from within ourselves. Not only remembered consciously, or recorded unconsciously, but etched into our very protoplasm. Genetically corroborated truths reminding us of what we once knew and what we once were. And, since what we once knew has remained within us all along, to read them is to learn again of ourselves.

"This is the book of the generations of man . . ." (Gen. 5:1) teaches us that on the day of the creation of human consciousness, the One of Being showed humanity all the generations, each with its leaders and sages and fools, yet to be. Still unable to leave the river of light, in which there is no past or future, and enter our cultured land of the ego, infant humanity beheld all of time. Says the myth, it is not that Adam understood the future, "He literally saw with his eyes the form in which future generations were destined to exist in the world."[24] "All the generations destined to come forth from him, standing and rejoicing before him."[25] "Nor can it be thought that after he saw them they disappeared, for all God's creations exist before Him permanently until they descend below."[26]

There is a "place" from which all places can be seen. And a "time" from which all times might be beheld. This place is in us and was once shown to us even as it is still within us to this day. Humanity's mythologies are replete with "memories" of having once been in this place, even as they all sadly likewise recount our amnesia of it. This place precedes life in this world and yet exists simultaneously with it. Its knowledge remains sealed in us.

Humanity once beheld the One of Being. All our sacred legends echo this truth. God showed humanity all the generations yet to come. The first human being (and each subsequent human being) for a moment understood about being part of the *Adam Kadmon,* the primordial person. And thus forever became a living record of all creation. A record that is apt to be summoned by the most trivial event and witnessed again.

It is not surprising that Abraham covers his eyes to keep from seeing Adam, even as he recognizes the first human parent. He knows the cave. Remembers the story. Understands that he is a character in Adam's story even as Adam is a character in his. Thus are parent and child at least for a moment reconciled.

Embryos, it is widely known, reenact evolutionary history. During our fetal development we are unicellular. We are fish, and fowl. And we are primates. We *are* those things. When the therapist says to the dreamer, "Be everything in your dream," he might also add, "because you were, and potentially are, those creatures." As it is said, ontogeny recapitulates phylogeny.

This genetic memory seems replete with all our ancestral forms. We can summon more than visual images. Not only can cells, returned to a neutral culture, lose their specific characteristics and revert to their original undifferentiated formlessness, but they also carry the potential reenactment of every evolutionary from through which (or whom) they have passéd. Experimental embryologists, for instance, have been able to retrieve from chicken cells a long-forgotten memory for forming teeth. The code, the memory, is perhaps not erased, only repressed, forgotten, recorded over.[27] The mystery is why one bit of protoplasm has a clear "informing" memory of how to create a human cornea, repressing everything else, while another seems obsessed with making feathers.

And in the same way that each cell carries within it the complete genotype for the entire organism, so each human being carries the whole story of creation. As each one of us is thus creation's museum, so too we are also its potential reenactment. Paddy Chayevsky's novel *Altered States* explores what such an existence might mean.[28] Each person can relive all creation. We can return through our phylogeny back through childhood and parents, mammals, amphibians, and protozoan slime, through volcanoes and cosmic debris to the act of creation itself. This legacy, this story, is insinuated in our molecular structure. There is a kind of super-primeval DNA-like code inscribed in the stuff of all being and we may, if we dare, become aware of it. The *Adam Kadmon*, the primordial human archetype, is more than just a legend. It is an ever-present possibility.

All material and all energy, perhaps, is likewise originally and therefore potentially unspecified. Everything able to become anything. "Among the archetypal memories and myths of our human origins are others that go much further back—back all the way to the ancestral clay, and perhaps even on into interstellar spaces. They have always been there, biding their time, waiting for the tide, surfacing now and then, sending shivers of mingled delight and dismay through phenotypes sentient enough to be sensitive to them. . . ."[29]

Even ordinary memory is not confined to one part of the brain. It has no exclusive place. Rather, it seems that remembering can be done by different cells and in different ways. It is fluid. Like light, it is simply everywhere it can be. Psychoneurologist Karl Lashly has found that memory storage is funneled between our two cerebral hemispheres. Whatever memory is, it is somehow able to be "stored" in different places and perhaps in different ways. Memory is not so much a "chip" as it is the way in which the letters are stored. Even the very notion of "storage" may turn out to be misleading materialism. "Human memory," reports W. L. Estes, "does not, in a literal sense, store anything; it simply changes as a function of experience."[30]

We simply remember more than we know. Every cell, every gene, every strand of DNA, every molecule, every atom, every electron, every photon. Each one of these is a little piece of memory. If a subatomic particle can carry a positive or negative electric charge, then it can be an element within a binary knowing system. A "yes" or a "no." Our most sophisticated computers are cumbersome attempts on the part of humanity to become aware of itself. We sense, with some dim amphibian urge, that we carry within ourselves the answer which we are "programmed" to finally become aware of.

There is some mysterious yearning within us that is convinced that we carry within us the answer which the very question of our life sets before us. And the beginning of the answer is already within the one who is wise enough to ask. We know it in the same way we know a dream we have dreamt and forgotten. Puzzled by our own curiosity, we compulsively return again to the "scene of the crime." But a fiery, ever-turning sword guards the way back to the tree of life (Gen. 3:24).

The stories never happen "out there." They constantly issue from us, with or without our conscious consent. They are in us and grow from us. The organizing structure of consciousness. They spring up from our depths, with only the slightest provocation. Biologically, they are already part of us. As there is in each cell a double helix of DNA determining the form and the function of that little bit of protoplasm, so there is in each person a double coiled spiral of stories, as it were. Something happens, and to our great surprise it turns out to have been "once upon a time." The genetic transmission of memory.

Consciousness informs matter. Matter is but another manifestation of consciousness. Mind and body are not two discrete realms but different expressions of the same underlying being. All awareness is thus also a bodily thing.

The developing mind contains an intuitive awareness of the origin and interconnectedness (and therefore the meaning) of the universe. It is not that we know the history of life and the history of the universe before life; we are made of it. It is made of us. In one mythic tradition there is a lost book called *Sefer Toldot HaAdam,* the Book of the Generations of Humanity (Gen. 5:1). It is not lost. It is not even misplaced. It is in us. We are the Book of the Generations of Humanity.

## THE STRUCTURE OF BEING

There is another way to imagine Adam. The primordial human being has a meta-human form. One that consists of an arrangement of relations and rhythms. One that begins from the inside and moves to the surface. Viewed from within we do not find familiar limbs, organs, and features. Instead of the external "what," there is an internal "why." Everything moves. Some things are so slow that they seem motionless. Others are so fast that we do not even see them as they go by. This is because vision is limited by our eyes. They have what is called a critical fusion frequency, which enables us to see only events that happen no faster than fifty times a second. (Motion pictures, for example, have only twenty-four still frames each second.[31]) What matters here, inside Adam, inside us, is the way in which everything moves and relates. Speed. Rhythm. Pulse. Arrangement and relationship. Here is the root of each creature's identity and the source of life. But this can only rarely be seen. It is concealed, it moves too fast, it moves too slow. We must therefore resort to symbolic diagrams. "Life is not in proteins, but in the music written on it; in its ability to recognize other molecules and to hold ordinary atoms in an extraordinarily precise way. . . . Form is the shaping force of life. All form or shape contains information . . . in the very configuration of our molecules and cells is the essence of our identity."[32]

According to the Kabbala, the primordial human being may accurately and alternately be portrayed as a person (all humanity or each one of us); a living tree; an arrangement of circles and spheres representing the primary forms of psychic energy and connected to one another by a network of channels; or, ultimately, as the inner structure of being itself—the psyche of the Holy One of Being. On one side of the structure there is the masculine principle, on the other, the feminine. Through the axis, the mediating principle. At the top is the unknowable and the infinite. Then there is cognition, a balance of (feminine) intuition and (masculine) insight. Below this are the two limbs, justice and mercy. In the very center is one point of harmony. There are organs of reproduction. There are feet, planted on the earth. Our humanity is not from our substance or even our parts, but from their inner dynamic, their motion, their relationship. The stuff of being is essentially neutral, dependent on where it is and who is around it.

The cells themselves are determined in their form and function by their relationship to one another. Their place in the arrangement of the whole organism defines their substance. "If a living cell is removed from its natural environment in the body and placed in a culture fluid in which it can grow and multiply, it often loses the characteristics of the organ it came from and becomes more or less similar to the undifferentiated cells from the early embryo."[33] We in the macrocosm are likewise determined. Position is everything in life.

Adam can also be understood as a tree. Its roots draw nourishment from the soil and serve as an anchor. The trunk holds it high to the sun. Powerful suction draws water and nutrients up from the roots. Branches spreading forth a great canopy. Leaves turned upward to gather in the light and transform it into edible energy. Tiny seeds, each carrying the blueprint of another tree, "after its kind," fall to the forest floor. The whole tree is in motion. And thus to tell of the tree must somehow communicate, in a motionless moment, something that is not still. As Buber once asked, shall we cut it down so as to still the movement?[34] But if we do, surely it will lie there and at once become the table for countless creatures and organisms who will continue the motion. Returning it to soil. But the soil too is alive. And even its inorganic minerals are themselves in motion.

This idea of the formative power of the inner dynamic of relationships is also well-known to us from the behavior of groups of people. The stated purpose of a group, its constituent members, or even its environment are of relatively meager importance when measured against the way its members relate to one another. And its effectiveness, its viability, its life is a function of its balance, the relationship of its "organs" to one another, its inner arrangement of motion. Imagine ten people merely standing in some perfect relationship to one another. Symbolizing the infinity of elements in the universe. Bringing their separate selves into the correct arrangement, the way the Creator meant for Adam to be. This Adam now broken. Parts no longer in the proper pattern. The One of Being also fragmented. Consciousness at odds with itself. Describing the theology of the *Zohar,* the central document of Jewish mysticism, David Blumenthal notes, "God's being is this consciousness and . . . this consciousness is a personalized anthropopathic consciousness whose elements are vitally interactive. . . . God's personality can, ostensibly, be destabilized by the actions of men."[35]

There is then some inner arrangement to being. One that is to reality what the crystalline structure of water is to each snowflake. If we understand the primary molecular pattern in the crystal, we are able to infer every particular snowflake yet to be. There is the structure of the carbon atom to organic life. The motif to a fugue. And a pattern to all being. But since the pattern is never still, it is more accurately called an arrangement of motions. Now whether or not this "arrangement of motions" describes only the inner workings of human consciousness or some primary infrastructure of being itself, we cannot say. We know only that we ourselves are in some sense creatures of being—creations of the One of Being—made by the same inner arrangement of motions and unable even to separate ourselves from being so as to form some detached, objective impression. (There is no such thing as "fantasy"; there are only symbols not yet understood.) In other words, it is not unreasonable that humanity's collective myths should reflect an accurate intuition of ultimate reality. "The structure of information in our cells is also the archetypal structure of information in the twistings and turnings of the species through time."[36]

In 1953, at the University of Chicago, a young biochemist named Stanley Miller conducted an awesome experiment. In brief, he set out to determine whether or not life could have originated on this planet according to what had been until that time only theory. He took the molecules assumed to have been plentiful in the earth's infant atmosphere: hydrogen, methane, ammonia, and water vapor—the incubating soup—mixed them in a kind of blender, and turned it on. He then subjected the spinning broth to regular electric charges, approximating as nearly as possible the action of lightning. By the end of a week the concoction had parented amino and nucleic acids, the building blocks of life.[37]

We wonder now from this respectful distance about the importance and the symbolic significance of lightning. Of sparks. Of light. Again and again it is the light that initiates. Light that rearranges the molecules so that they might produce life. "Let there be light." And how is it that the unknown author of the first creation account of Genesis knew to begin with light? Perhaps our penchant for returning to and reverencing lightning is—like the story of the great flood and amniotic waters—more like memory than fantasy. From whence could such wisdom come if not from beings who themselves are created by light? Filled with light. Made conscious by it.

Let us reconsider our story of creation. It is a legend that, like those of all the other traditions, from the beginning of the world to the end of the cave, begin and end the same way: in consciousness. Light.

# Chapter 5

# The Light
# of Creation

*And God said, Let there be light, and there was light. This is the original light which God created. It is the light of the eye. It is the light which God showed to Adam, and through which he was able to see from one end of creation to the other.*
—Zohar[1]


*In the beginning, consciousness rises up like an island with whatever contents it then has, but soon sinks back again into the unconscious. There is in fact no continuity of consciousness.*
—Eric Neumann[2]


*We may be utterly mistaken in the way we usually oppose the cosmology of the Bible to that of modern science. The laws of the universe that spiritual traditions speak of may be laws that can only be observed in a new state of consciousness. That is to say, they can only be observed when a man is aware of the movements of energy* within himself.
—Jacob Needleman[3]

*N*ow Abraham is able to see the light. *After following the calf. Finding the cave. Adam and Eve. Parents. His eyes have become accustomed to the darkness and he realizes that there is some other source of light. Shining through a pinhole into Eden from the other end of time. It is, of course, the river of light. It has a purity he has never seen before. With such light a person could see from one end of the world to the other. Nothing could remain concealed. Is this perhaps the meta-light whispered of in the legends? A light-like-consciousness by which being began? One that Adam saw but, because of infant humanity's moral unreliability, had to be hidden away for some future generation? "Light is sown for the righteous" (Ps. 97:11).*

*Here is the legend. The story of the light of the seven days of creation, the light of consciousness: the Light that was created on the first day was an awesome primordial light. Seven times brighter than the light of the sun, which was not created until day four. It was so bright that while the sun rose and set, there was never the sense of darkness or therefore of night.[4] The sun must have appeared then like the moon by day. This primordial light shone uninterrupted over the seven days of creation and was not concealed until the close of the seventh day —the conclusion of the first Sabbath, on Saturday evening. But once the sun of that first Sabbath had set, and coincident with it the concealment of the primordial light of creation, then a great and terrible darkness descended.*

*Now Adam, you will remember, had been created on the sixth day of the days of creation—according to midrashic tradition, Friday afternoon. It was on that day that he sinned. On that day he was judged and on that day he was banished from the garden. Nevertheless, he did not see darkness until the going out of the Sabbath, at sunset on Saturday evening, one day and a half after his creation.* [5]

*Alone in this new night he cried out, "Woe to me. For now that I have defiled the world, this darkness is come upon it forever. Creation will revert to primordial chaos. Heaven has condemned me to death." And so he sat in fasting and weeping all the night long. And Eve wept beside him. It was not until dawn broke (imagine it: the first real dawn!) that he realized the order of the universe. He then arose and offered the first sacrifice (and, we assume, thereby initiated what has come to be called organized religion).* [6]


## SCIENCE AND RELIGION

In order to study the work of creation we shall need to learn from humanity's two great truth traditions: science and religion. Their apparent disagreement is only the inevitable outcome of their different goals. Science tries to tell "what" and religion tries to answer "what for." As Huston Smith has suggested,[7] it is the difference between quantification and qualification. Science is concerned with the empirical, objective, external fact, and religion with the personal, subjective, internal experience. Science must therefore "religiously" exclude feelings, while religion must "scientifically" factor them in. In classical science, the person of the observer can only contaminate, while in religion it is this same "person" who is our only concern. This explains why the results should on the surface appear so contradictory.

Science moves forward. Religion backward. Science grows by integrating more and more information into intelligible systems of increasing quantity and simplicity. Moving through its own eras, punctuated by revolutions, science grows by outgrowing the previous era's arrangements of information. Religion, on the other hand, eternally rediscovers the ancient truth known in principle by the first beings (or Being), which over the generations has become increasingly obscured, concealed, and encrusted. Until there is a revival (not a revolution). Some teacher or school or sect says, "We have forgotten the primary truth." In the words of my teacher, Arnold Jacob Wolf, "The old lies are true!"

Remember: one who is able to reach a rung of consciousness utterly unaware of oneself and aware only of the "outside world" (science), and one who is able to reach a rung of consciousness utterly unaware of the outside world and aware only of one's innermost self (spirit) will have arrived at the same place. In telling "what," one cannot avoid answering "why," just as in answering "why," one necessarily implicates "what." And so it is that the traditions are very close.

The opening chapter of Genesis is, for instance, restored to its proper place of "religion's" importance if we permit it to answer the question of the purpose of human existence or the meaning of life. As such, it is an eloquent answer to humanity's eternal "why?" It does not aim to offer a "scientific" account of creation. It is unconcerned with what actually happened. And yet, by teaching of the purpose of being, it betrays a surprisingly accurate, almost empirical, memory of events it could not have possibly witnessed.

## THE POINT OF LIGHT

The first letter of the Hebrew Bible, *beit,* is the second letter of the Hebrew alphabet. The first letter of the alphabet, *aleph,* has virtually no sound at all. One might say, then, that there is nothing prior to the *beit* of creation. The letter *beit* itself, when prefixed to the beginning of a word, is a simple preposition meaning "in," "with," or "by." Now the first word of the Hebrew Bible, if we drop the first letter, *beit,* is *raysheet,* or, as it is commonly (but perhaps incorrectly) translated, "beginning." Variant traditions also render it as "Torah," in the sense of some preexistent wisdom or consciousness. One old festival prayerbook even has the Torah speak thus: "Long before any of His works, and long before the ancient things, I existed . . . when the world was water I existed; and while the world was chaos, I was then as a light. . . ." Hence we might now read the first verse of Genesis, "With Torah, God created the heavens and the earth. . . ."[8] But the *Zohar* is the most explicit:

> *In the beginning*—When the will of the King began to take effect, He engraved signs into the heavenly sphere (that surrounded Him). Within the most hidden recess a dark flame issued from the mystery of *Ayn Sof* . . . neither white nor black, neither red nor green, of no color whatever. Only after this flame began to assume size and dimension, did it produce radiant colors. From the innermost center of the flame sprang forth a well out of which colors issued and spread upon everything beneath. . . . It could not be recognized at all until a hidden, supernal point shone forth. . . . The primal center is the innermost light, of a translucence, subtlety, and purity beyond comprehension. . . . Beyond this point nothing can be known. Therefore it is called *raysheet,* beginning. . . .[9]

This *raysheet* point rises from a soundless, almost *aleph*-like nothingness of infinite creative potential. It is none other than the beginning point of being. With *raysheet,* the Holy One fashioned the heavens and the earth. Being began.

During the second decade of this century, astronomer Edwin Hubble noticed that light reaching us from distant galaxies contained a disproportionate amount of longer wave lengths. This phenomenon of stretching out the wave lengths shifted their observable color along the spectrum toward the red. In the same way, the whine of a car approaching us on a highway sounds high-pitched, and becomes lower as it moves away from us. This is because as the car approaches us, the sound waves are pushed together resulting in a higher sound. As the car moves away from us, the sound waves are drawn apart, resulting in a lower sound. In the case of light, this bunching up, or shortening, of wave lengths makes the light bluer, and when drawn apart, or lengthened, they appear redder. This is called the Doppler shift. Hubble posited that, since distant galaxies are shifted toward the red, they must be moving away from us (and from one another): the universe is expanding. Everything is moving away from everything else at tremendous speed. At some specific time in the past, then, all the galaxies and stars and planets and, indeed, space itself must have been concentrated into a much denser mass.

We might therefore reconstruct the early hours and minutes of the universe. The closer or denser things would get, the hotter it would become. Only the simplest and most stable atoms could endure the intense temperature and radiation. This fact would also explain the great preponderance of simple hydrogen atoms to more complicated and less stable molecules in the universe.[10]

As we move further back in time, crossing the threshold where the temperature exceeds 4000 degrees Kelvin, there would be so much radiation—pulsing waves of energy—that matter itself could not exist. There would instead be "only an ionized and undifferentiated soup. . . ."[11] An era of plasma [12]

Here subatomic particles—leptons, hadrons, quarks, photons— could not stay together long enough even to form atoms but instead would continually be created out of pure energy and, after short lives, annihilated again.[13] In this primordial furnace, the stuff of being began.

By the first 1/100 second, the universe was a hundred thousand million degrees centigrade with a density four thousand million times that of water. A primeval fireball growing smaller and smaller and smaller. The immense gravity draws into itself all the matter and all the energy until, as it approaches infinite density, the curvature of space and time would likewise be infinite. Nothing escapes. All being is drawn back into one dimensionless mathematical point of infinite density,[14] which Einstein would call a singularity. Not an object but an absurdity. A place where known physics comes to an end.[15]

> We must suppress our thoughts and refrain from seeking and exploring what is above and below, what is before and what is beyond. Rabbi Johanan deduced this in Rabbi Levi's name from the fact that the first letter of the Torah is a *beit,* shaped thus ב. This teaches that just as the *beit* is closed on all sides and open on one side only, so must you not inquire what is above or below (the universe), what was before creation and what will be after.[16]

Before the *beit* of *b'raysheet,* before the point of light, there was no before. For there was no time in which before could have been.


## A HOVERING PRESENCE

The second verse of the creation legend speaks of void and nothingness. The universe was *tohu va-vohu,* primeval chaos. Darkness even darker than unconsciousness on the face of the abyss. But now the growing point of being's awareness begins to light up the blackness. The spirit of the Holy One hovers over the waters —like a dove fluttering over her nest.[17] A soft hum filling the airless sky. Waiting there wanting only to become aware. To get on with the business of creation.

In 1965, in Holmdel, New Jersey, two radio astronomers named Arno Penzias and Robert Wilson set out to measure the radio waves emitted from our galaxy. By aiming the mechanical ear of a twenty-foot horn reflector of an ultra low noise radio telescope in different directions, and comparing the noise they received with the virtually motionless noise of liquid helium, they would be able to determine source and filter out static. Expecting very little electrical noise, they began listening at relatively short wavelengths.

No matter where or when they listened, Penzias and Wilson kept picking up microwave radiation background noise equivalent to 3.5° Kelvin. Everywhere in the universe there was this hum. But it was only when cosmologists took seriously the implications of the "big bang" cosmogony that they realized what Penzias and Wilson had discovered. If the universe had begun from one point with this great bang, then as it expanded its once equivalent temperature of billions upon billions upon billions of degrees would be lowered over the aeons to a predictable few degrees Kelvin. And it would appear naturally as background noise coming equally from all directions.[18] This static, fossil-like radiation, then, was the most ancient signal ever received by astronomers.[19] None other than the ember-fading-glow of the primeval fireball itself. A feeble, dwindling hum of the moment of creation.

The echo of one electromagnetic chord that is the sound of creation. It is soft. Perhaps the softest sound next to no sound there could be. But it can be heard. Heard by each generation. Flickering toward us from long-since-fled galaxies. Through the air we breathe. A sound that seems to issue through the molecules of breathing bodies and inorganic matter. A kind of hovering in which we talk and imagine and see. Perhaps, in the medium of consciousness, the cosmic microwave radiation of creation's sound persists. But, because we have never heard its "silence" go off— as we do not notice the refrigerator's hum until it stops—we do not know what it sounds like.

There is preserved in the rhythmic pulse of subatomic particles called photons, a faint sound of the very first moments. And if memory is some kind of record from which we can draw at will —the universe hums with a kind of memory of its own genesis. And the sound of the Holy One of Being hovering over the face of the waters can still be heard even unto this very day.

## THE SPECTRUM OF BEING

And it is then, from this hovering presence over the waters, that the One of Being says, "Let there be Light." And with the same simple mystery that thought becomes speech or that intention becomes action or that energy becomes matter, "there was Light." Not a second idea or the next step but all part of the flow of one sentence. (The divisions between phrases and words and letters are a human invention.) Here the "Let there be" and the "And there was" are both of one totality. As the flame is joined to the burning coal, so the intention is joined to the creation.

Consciousness alters the physical universe. The Newtonian, everyday, cause and effect, determinist, material world, which has room only for billiard balls and the laws that predict how they move, is violated by the Holy One of Being who speaks "Let there be" as well as by ordinary physicists who, by observing their experiments, alter the results. It is a "word" that does not cause but rather is synchronous with its creation: "And there was." At least in the beginning, thought, word, and consciousness are the same as thing, world, and creation. Materialism and idealism dissolve into one another. The work of the first day is not just "light" but the "and God spoke" that occurs at the same moment. And it is this consciousness and its creation together that give birth to day and night. One day. Underlying the endurance of this world is the One who says, "Let there be Light." Beneath this world a consciousness-like-light glistens. At bottom, consciousness and matter are one.

In the late nineteenth century, James Clerk Maxwell was able to integrate theories of electricity, magnetism, and light into one general formulation. Subsequent generations of scientists would discover and add such phenomena as radio waves and gamma rays to fill out the entire (electromagnetic) spectrum. X-rays and radar, heat and radio waves, and visible light are now understood as bands of a larger whole. Differing in frequency and wavelength, but substantially the same. (Take the wavelike particles—the particlelike waves—that register on our optic nerves as yellow, move them up and down faster, alter the distance between the crests of each wave, and you can make a gamma ray or a radio wave.) Einstein demonstrated that matter itself is yet only another form of energy. That the structure of space and time was itself connected to and curved by gravity. Here is the vision of a new kind of physics working toward a "unified field," in which all manifestations of reality are "scientifically" interrelated. And physicist John Archibald Wheeler, in his theory of geo-metrodynamics, has suggested that matter is actually a disturbance in the underlying structure of space-time.[20]

Where do we fall on the spectrum? We have not yet been able to place the consciousness of the one who is arranging and observing the spectrum itself. The one who watches the unfolding of creation. And the one who speaks and the experiment begins. (And surely the One who spoke and being began.)

Descartes "set humanity aside from nature, and established criteria of 'rational objectivity' for natural science that placed the scientist himself in the position of a pure spectator. . . ."[21] It was not until Werner Heisenberg, one of the first generation of quantum physicists, that the scientific observer could—indeed had to—return to the experiment. Heisenberg discovered that "our acts of observation alter the states of the particles we observe."[22] Human consciousness itself must unavoidably be placed on the spectrum of being. In the words of Nobel physicist Eugene Wigner, "consciousness is the primary reality."[23]

According to what Heisenberg called the uncertainty principle, detached objective observation—on the most primary and subatomic levels—was not possible. In the very act of "observing" an event we invariably change it. The reflected waves by which we "observe" anything and within/by whose medium we are conscious in the first place, change/interact with/alter what we had hoped to watch "secretly." Observer becomes participant. All being, from space to time, matter to energy, intention to creation, is on one spectrum. Or, more correctly, different facets of the one underlying reality.

Matter is no longer matter but patterns of energy. Radiation, like light, is perhaps itself only a transient form of consciousness. In such a way the consciousness of "let there be" can actually translate into "and there was." Consciousness fashions cosmos.

The mystery, then, is not so much that intention and word, mind and matter, space and time can "affect one another," but why we seem to perceive them as being discrete at all. The continum of being extends through all the manifestations of being including human "beings." Our consciousness, that elusive, still unexplainable (apparent) dimension of ourselves, and perhaps (probably, unquestionably) our hallmark and "reason" for being is to matter and time as red is to blue and yellow. It is as simple as "And the One spoke"—and "there was." In the words of one of the most eloquent contemporary exponents of this "spectrum of being," William Irwin Thompson: "The universe is not a black box containing floating bits of junk left over from the big bang explosion; it is a consciousness saturated solution. Mind is not simply located in the human skull; animal, vegetable, and mineral forms are all alive."[24] Is this process called consciousness somehow fundamentally the same as what we also call light?

## THE LIGHT OF CONSCIOUSNESS

The first creation was light. It is, as Ernst Cassirer has shown, a metaphor for consciousness raising itself from the dark oblivion of unconsciousness.[25] The One of Being brought forth consciousness from the primeval chaos of unawareness. Might this be true not only for the psychic history of the individual (ontogeny), as Cassirer's thoughtful reading of creation mythology teaches, but also as a literal insight into the origin of the universe itself (phylogeny)?

What we ordinarily call light is but a relatively narrow band of waves of radiation near the center of the electromagnetic spectrum.[26] This phenomenon is doubtlessly due to the fact that most of the sun's radiation is also of the same frequency. Most life on earth has consequently evolved so as to make maximum use of it. But, of course, there is much more to light than meets the eye. Such electromagnetic energy, in its broadest sense, pulses within all being, possibly including consciousness itself. Light then might be more than just a metaphor for consciousness. And when Genesis "remembers" that the first utterance of the Holy One was, "Let there be light," it may know more than it lets on. (Dreams do, on occasion, partake of eternal truths.) This might also explain our fascination with this light-like-consciousness and our equal inability to comprehend it.

We seem condemned to (re)discover time after time that you cannot behold that of which you are made without ceasing to be who you are. Before people are born and after they die they "behold a great light." But not as long as they remain who they are. We are part of what we seek to study. Philo similarly has observed, "As in the case of light, which can only be seen by means of light, so too, God is not to be conceived except through Him: 'The questers after truth are they who envisage God by means of God, light by means of light.' "[27] "A photon, the ultimate unit of Light (consciousness), can be seen only once; its detection is its annihilation. Light is not seen; it is seeing."[28] This paradox is expressed in the description of the photon, the fundamental subatomic "particle" of all radiation. It is a particle without mass. Neither a wave nor a thing. Nevertheless, packets or "quanta" of them make up the waves and the motions that seem to be the infrastructure of being. Are they not perhaps what is spoken of in the myth as the hidden Light of the first "days" of creation?

Here, in the consideration of light, the truth traditions of science and religion converge. It is a no-place of no quantification and no qualification. Where mind and matter meet. A mode of being within all creation. The underlying river of consciousness itself. On some subatomic level so obscure that philosophers still have as much permission to be there as physicists, matter and energy converge. If it is not in the massless "particle" of the photon, then in some nothing else. Some arrangement of motion that must look to the eye like light. And which mythic spiritual traditions call by that same name. And which human beings experience in moments of self-reflection as consciousness. It is more than the ordinary light that illumines this page, which is nothing more than a gross metaphor. It is the light of consciousness that was hidden away after the first week of creation.

The *Zohar* too knows this, for it reminds us that this first-day light preceded the fourth-day creation of the sun. "The original light which God created . . . this is the light of the eye. It is the light which God showed to Adam, and through which he was able to see from one end of being to the other. . . . Rabbi Isaac said . . . The light was hidden away in order that the wicked of the world might not enjoy it and it is treasured up for the righteous. . . . 'Light is sown for the righteous' "(Ps. 107:11).[29] This Light is called the *or ganooz.* The light stored within.

This finds an analogue in recent cosmological theory. We understand that in the very early universe, above the temperature threshold of 4000° Kelvin, energy itself was not, as it is now, contained in the masses of atomic particles, but in the form of radiation.[30] There were then at least two distinct eras. The first era was dominated by radiation. Pulsing electromagnetic waves of energy everywhere. "The roar of light." Light more than sunlight with no eye to behold. But as the winter chill of our present cosmos set in, the second era began. This one is dominated by gross matter. Material substance containing trapped light. We feel it in our bones. There is even a tradition in the Lurianic Kabbala that tells of holy sparks or *nitzotzot* imprisoned in everything. Yearning to be set free through the agency of human intention and deed.[31]

Picture them for a moment. Transitory bits of light. Annihilated in an instant. Reflected needles of sunlight on the ripples of water. Sparks. Present now and then they are gone. Left over from the creation event. Caught now inside everything and everyone. A light-like consciousness. Echoing the beginning. Hovering just above at 3° Kelvin. Somewhere between spirit and matter. Hidden away in galaxies and trees and you and me. Shimmering. Like sunlight on water that will not be still. Set before us.

There is a legend of a second kind of Light. Saturday evening, after the withdrawal of the primordial Light (of consciousness) and the setting of the sun, Adam was left in utter darkness. It was then that he rubbed the first stones together and initiated fire: humanity's response to its own darkness and exile. Its way of "making it through the night." Its weak yet indispensable light. Fire is manmade consciousness. Fire is humanity's attempt to endure unredeemed creation. In much the same way that everything must pass through the nothingness on its way to becoming something else, so too is fire the symbol for material transformation. The chemical reaction through which the sacrifice becomes an offering and matter becomes energy. "Command the children of Israel to bring you the pure oil of beaten olives for lighting; to keep a light going continually" (Lev. 24:2).

Its control is not only evidence of human uniqueness but symbolic of organized religion. When the "light" was withdrawn, when we were left alone without the immediate awareness of the Holy One, we were able to make do with religion. It is a kind of stop-gap measure until the final reunification.

"Rabbi Samuel bar Nahman said: In this world people walk in the light of the sun by day and the light of the moon by night, but in the time to come they will not walk by the light of the sun by day or the light of the moon by night. . . . And by whose light will they walk? By the light of the Holy One."[32]

It is as if the primary act of creation is simply becoming conscious, and that through becoming conscious we—like God—create ourselves. The first and most important creation that human beings (and through them the One of Being) and the One of Being (and through the One of Being, human beings) can give birth to is consciousness. Awareness. Eyes open, remade for wonder. Eyes that see. Ears that hear. Hands that feel. Breathless for a moment we behold the dawn. The first light. An idea dawns. And what was nothing comes into being. Let there be Light.

Humanity, one might say, is the organ of consciousness in the universe. We are the result of consciousness's desire to become aware of itself. As Jung observed, "If the Creator were conscious of himself, he wouldn't have needed us."[33] Being speaks of and listens to itself through humanity. Our wickedness is creation's perversion. Our vision, creation's hope. If all existence is one organism, then humanity is its eyes and ears, its hands and its heart. The universe is sentient because we are part of the universe and we are sentient. Human awareness is as empirical and incontrovertible a fact as gravity or photosynthesis. Our amazement, our tears, our intuitions, and our silences are part of being. And for us to call the cosmos insensate would be like our eyes surveying our body and calling it blind.

Of course there is no consciousness in the universe without humanity. Humanity is the organ of consciousness in the universe. And for this reason we hold our Creator hostage; without our eyes, the Holy One of Being would be blind. Insensate. Bumping into galaxies. Compelled to begin all over again with some other (unsuspecting) genetic line. When we see, it is not only for ourselves. Another One sees through our seeing. Peering through the lattice. Another One stands behind us. A river of light flows within.


A consciousness-like-light wells up through and creates each order of being. Atomic particles. Atoms. Molecules. Minerals. Plants. Animals. Humanity. In an inexorable desire to become aware of itself. Each one of us, beings of light that we are, carry these layers in our psyche, our genes. Our very protoplasm. Go down through your layers, through your childhood and your dreams. Through the apes and the amphibians and the fish and the protozoan slime. Through the volcanic waters and the carbon dioxide on down to the light-like-consciousness by which being began and by whose still soft hum we are blessed to breathe and wonder. It is a spiritual ontogeny recapitulating a metaphysical phylogeny. For the layers run back through time but also run all the way down to the source, at any given moment. The fish and the volcano and the light are in us now.

At the beginning of being there is light: the light of the first day, which preceded the sun. And at the height of consciousness there is light: the light that is treasured away for the righteous ones. From this light we emerge into the world and to it we return. Since all being emanated from it, we cannot "see" it. And therefore it "appears" (to the part of our thinking entrusted with making analytic sense) as nonsense, or simply as nothing at all. Yet humanity, refusing to believe the evidence right before its eyes, stubbornly, in each generation, through the word of sacred myth or the hands of trusted technology, returns again and again to the spirit. The searching for the light.

When we return to creation thus, we reenter a mode of consciousness in which consciousness and its "object" are the same.

But as we saw (learned) at Sinai—to become conscious of our own consciousness is impossible. At least in our present evolutionary form. Our next shape and our final shape will be as beings of pure light.[34] Pure consciousness. A shape that has for ages been described as Nothingness. To become aware of the work of creation —back through light which we see, to light (radiation) which is more than we can see, on to the soft pulsing echo of creation, back to the nothing point of the origin/Genesis of all being—is to become ourselves nothing.

# Chapter 6

# Returning to Nothing

*They then said that each of them should tell an old story, the story which represented the earliest thing that he could remember, from that very point where his memory began. There were both old and young people there, and they gave to the eldest among them the honor of beginning. He said: "What can I tell you? I remember when they cut the apple from the branch." No one quite understood what he meant by that, but the wise men agreed that this was indeed a very ancient memory. The second elder, who was just a bit younger than the first, was then given the honor. "Is that an old tale?" he said. "I remember that one too, but I also remember when the candle was yet burning." They agreed that this memory was older than the first, but were puzzled to find that it was the younger man who had the older memory. They then called upon the third, who was still younger. "I remember," he said, "when the fruit first began to be formed." They agreed that this was a still older memory. The fourth, who was yet younger, said "I remember when they carried the seed to plant the fruit." The fifth claimed that he remembered the sages who contemplated the seed. The sixth remembered the taste of the fruit before it entered the fruit. The seventh remembered the aroma before it entered the fruit, and the eighth recalled its appearance in that same way. And I (said the blind beggar who was telling all this) was yet a child, but I was there too. I said to them: "I remember all these events. But I also remember nothing* (Ikh gedenk gor nisht)." *And they answered: "This is indeed an older memory than all."*

—*Rabbi Nahman of Bratslav*[1]

*All right. My matter was returning to pure energy, to a condition of pure nothingness. And you saved me from nothingness . . . you see, matter, energy, our whole universe, are not absolutes. They are all fictions of human consciousness . . . the beginning of life . . . is nothing, simple hideous nothing!*

—*Paddy Chayevsky*[2]

*A* braham follows the light to its apparent source. But this light, which originates in the Garden, is bright beyond mere seeing. It is a light of such intensity that its own brilliance cannot escape it. The waves are turned inward and back upon themselves. In the distant heavens it might appear as a black hole. In the consciousness of the aged patriarch there must have likewise been a similar brush with oblivion.

We do not know what it is like at the other end of that cave of Machpelah. Or we do not remember. Beyond the Garden of Eden, surely still drenched in the shimmering plasma light of some earlier consciousness, there can be no ordinary syntax. And yet it is a place not limited to before birth and after death. Abraham went there and returned. And what happens to the parents is, if not a promise, then at least a possibility for the children.

We know only from our version of this journey toward consciousness that the old man returned, having chosen this cave as his burial place. Those who have survived near-death experiences likewise report seeing a great light. Whether his appearance was altered or his awareness transformed we do not know. The Bible maintains its majestic silence. All we know is that somehow, on account of this journey, this accidental (?) discovery, he had selected this cave as a burial site for himself; he was now willing (able?) to contemplate his own death. Now prepared to consider the annihilation of his own ego. For some reason, which we

*can only intuit as being correct, the other side of the light of this ultimate*
*primordial consciousness is nothingness. The sequence before us is in this case,*
*as in all the other parallels: death, transformation, and rebirth. In a word,*
*Nothingness.*

## NOTHINGNESS

Not enough has been said in our generation of God's Nothingness. I do not mean the Nothingness spoken of by the nihilists who believe, with a kind of disappointed piety, that the ultimate reality is actually nothing. Nor do I mean the Nothingness of the classical mystics who knew of the self's utter dissolution into the infinity. I mean, instead, the Nothingness that lies just beyond every something as its ultimate expression and transformation into another something: the beginning of being. And the end of being. You cannot become someone other than you are until you are willing, for just one moment, to allow yourself to become one whom you are not. That is, until you are willing to enter the Nothing. It is possibly the most effortless (and the most important) thing any of us can do.

The great Maggid of Mezritch taught it this way: nothing can simply change from one reality into another without first attaining the level of Nothingness. An egg must first cease to exist as an egg before the chick can come forth from it. So it is with everything in the world. Even miracles that seem to alter the natural order must first bring nature itself into the Nothingness. Only then can the miracle come forth.[3]

This is the Nothingness that, of necessity, joins every something. When the children of Israel left Egypt they passed through this Nothingness and were transformed by it. They had to quit being who they were, slaves, and for a moment (it must have seemed like an eternity) endure their own death. Withstand their own transformation. Emerge, reborn, as free people on the other side of the sea. In the words of Exodus 14:29, "They went into the midst of the sea on dry ground." There was a moment for them when two things that cannot coexist coexisted. They were in the midst of the sea. Yet they were on dry ground. It did not become dry ground until they set foot in the sea. They did not become free until slaves did what only free people can do.

This is logically unintelligible. A thing and its contradiction. Sea and dry ground. Slave and free. Consciousness collapses under its own weight. The left cerebral hemisphere can no longer endure the madness of it all and tells us that, when a thing and its opposite are the same, the logical result is everything and Nothing. Just this is the last place of our awareness after it has ceased to be what it was but before it has become what it will next be.

In a way, all the great mythic moments are like this. Sinai, for instance. How could God, who is infinite, speak to people who are finite without destroying them both? You will recall the many legends that suggest that everyone at first did indeed die! Or the story of the creation event. How could something come from nothing? (Such an incomprehensible assertion the dogmaless Jews elevated to an article of faith anyway.) How could light come forth from darkness? Consciousness from unconsciousness? Or the legend of the great redemption at the Red Sea. How could a people go into the midst of the sea on dry ground? It is almost as if, in order to fully grasp the meaning of the story, our own consciousness must endure that same nothingness that spans the distance between death and rebirth. (Only by allowing yourself to relive the story can you experience what cannot be understood. "In every generation, each Jew must experience himself as though he personally were freed from Egypt.")[4]

Every religious moment participates in this Nothingness. Rehearsals for the times of transformation. Religion helps us to endure them. It schools us in their transforming power. And the Holy One of Being would then be the One whom we meet during the passage. This God is King over a realm of Nothingness. This One stands just beyond the edge of the void and says only to we who are huddled on the shore, unable to retreat, afraid to go forward, "It is time now." And we, from time to time, when we allow ourselves to relive the great religious myths, step into the midst of the sea—on what turns out to be dry ground. We enter the Nothingness. It happens at least every seventh day.

## THE SEVENTH DAY

"On the seventh day God ceased from work and took a breath" (Exod. 31:17).[5] Consider the Nothingness of simply being open. Empty. Not hollow or glazed or silent. Able to hear what incessantly springs up from the emptiness within. Like an unending procession of clowns coming out of a tiny car at the circus. We listen with amazement to the voices that seem to speak from nowhere. Not hallucinations or fantasies, but words streaming from our mouths, words we did not know were in us to utter. The rarely perceived, unfathomable, ever-flowing river inside—when we are empty—uses our mouths as its vessel.

The definitive mark of this doing nothing is that there can be no previous motive. No earlier agenda. When we eat we only eat. When we speak we only speak. When we walk we only walk. We can walk somewhere, but the destination is not as important as the walking. If, for example, I am going to the doctor now, and this is the reason for the walking, then the walking and the destination are inseparable. They are one act. There is an inner unity to everything we do—or for that matter, don't do. There is nothing before. Nothing after.

The paradigm expression of this in Judaism is Shabbat. For one-seventh of our weekly universe we are bidden not to rest, but to *do* Nothing. Shabbat is a day that not only communicates how something came from Nothing, but how something can also return to Nothing. On the seventh day the world is just as it is. For six days I have toiled to fix it. Change it. Make it. Now I declare that, however it is, it is Nothing. I abandon all motives. Whether hidden or revealed. For six days I have done everything I have done for some antecedent motive or some yet unfulfilled reason. On the seventh day I mimic the One who spoke the first letter that had no sound: I do nothing. Whatever I do I do for no reason, other than the simple Nothing fact that I am doing it. Since everything is done—at least according to the spiritual fiction by which I abide —then there is nothing to do. And whatever I do can then only come from Nothing. And since it can therefore only lead to Nothing, I am free from the past and the future. And whatever issues from me can only be from Nothing.

And when the day of Nothing is done I return to my work. Being again defined by something ulterior to itself. Oriented toward some goal. But I nevertheless remember the Sabbath just past or the one about to come. And in such a way, my work is transformed too. For this reason, it is said, that were all Israel to keep but one Sabbath, the Messiah could tarry no longer.


This inner unity is called serving God with a whole heart. Doing only "for the sake of Heaven." There are two ways of attaining this place which has no place. One is the way of the East, self-annihilation. To empty oneself of all self until, through being absolutely nothing, one becomes all. The other way is according to the way of the West, self-realization. Here the aim is to comprehend and tend the world. To fill oneself with the self of the universe and in so doing to become everything (which is also nothing). Both ways, the way of the East and the way of the West, are only the yin and the yang. The end of each path is Nothing.

The Maggid of Mezritch was a great teacher of Nothing. He explained that

> The work of the pious is greater than the creation of the heavens and the earth.[6] For while the creation of the heavens and the earth was making something from Nothing, the pious transform something into Nothing. Through everything that they do, even with mundane acts like eating, they raise the holy sparks which are within the food back to heaven. And thus with everything we realize that they transform something into Nothing.[7]

The Holy One of Being, whom we sense was once everything and everywhere, created the heavens and earth out of this oneness. Human beings who have learned how to serve Heaven with their every action—and on account of this are called pious—are able to "raise" everything they touch back to its highest original source: Nothing. They do not annihilate it. They do not destroy its existence. They complete it. It seems, therefore, that the Holy One of Being is both the source and the destiny of the heavens and the earth. The first seed and the last seed of all creation. The Nothingness that bore us and that in the end will receive us. The One who uttered the first soundless *Aleph* with which the self-reflection of consciousness began. The One whose mere intention to raise that awareness above the dumb gracefulness of unconsciousness began creation. And the One whose very Nothingness will transform our consciousness yet again and again. Now consciousness was not, of course, spoken of as such until recently; tradition instead arranged a hierarchy of the Names of God.


## THE HIERARCHY OF CONSCIOUSNESS

"And I appeared to Abraham, to Isaac, and to Jacob as *Ael Shaddai* but by my Name *Yod Hey Vav Hey*, I was not known to them" (Exod. 6:3).[8] So God has more than one name. There may even be hundreds. But they do not tell very much about God. Instead, they describe the ones who give, and who use, and who hope in the Name. This is all the history of theology. Desert nomads call upon a wandering patriarch. Landed priests—an enthroned King. And student sages, an ultimate teacher. There are Names that are appropriate to a certain liturgy. During the days of penitence, God is "Our Father, Our King." But when called during the morning blessings, God is the "Creator of Light." And it is now fashionable to read Scripture as the layered patchwork of several documents, each one having its own God (Name). The *Yod Hey Vav Hey* name is purportedly favored by the "J" author and *Elohim* by the "E" author. But the Holy One of Being is, of course, beyond all names. Beyond even the mystical *Temira D'Temirin*, "Hidden of the Hidden." Remaining forever the Nameless One. Leaving us alone with "our" names, which, on occasion, correspond to the levels of our own spiritual consciousness and psychological development. They can be arranged on a hierarchy; at the bottom is power.

## The Name of Power

At the beginning of religious consciousness is a God who is very much like us (or at least like we would like to be) and deals with us accordingly. With a God like this you make a covenant. This is the one called *Elohim* or *Ael Shaddai*. Here belong the personal, intimate, anthropomorphic names. On an internal level this is a child's nascent consciousness now struggling to fathom the power and simple reality of those who surround us. Those with whom we must enter into commerce. Those who must be placated, trusted, understood, feared, loved. Above this bottom level is the Lord of Being whose name is Being.

## The Name of Being

Hebrew is not customarily written with vowels. The little dots and lines below and after the consonants—while indispensable to the student—are a later invention. Proper pronounciation of the consonants in a Hebrew word requires seeing it in its context. One must understand the drift of the sentence in order to read it correctly. Meaning, in other words, preceeds sound. (It is not as impossible as it all seems. Like other semitic languages, Hebrew words are built from roots, usually three letters. Whenever these three consonants appear in the same sequence, they convey the same "root" idea. The context will tell the reader what particular sense of the root idea is meant.)

*Yod, hey, vav.* Three letters in this language of no vowels that sometimes function as vowels. The letter *yod* can indicate vowels of the "ay" and "ee" class. *Hey,* those of the "ah" and "aw" sound. And *vav,* the vowel sounds of "oh" and "oo." These letters focus and refine the sounds of consonants. They have no substance of their own. Living in the spaces just after each letter. They are the ether in which consonants linger, and the medium of meaningful sound. Necessary for all pronunciation and communication, yet having not enough sound-substance of their own to stand by themselves. More like the universal noises of human emotion. Sounds like breathing, exhaustion, and ecstasy. These then are, not surprisingly, the letters of the root of the word for being itself. The verb "to be."

These also are the letters of the Name of God: *Yod, Hey, Vav, Hey.* The Holy One of Being. The ineffable Name of Being. The Tetragrammaton. A Name that, by ancient religious convention, and by our very physiological structure, cannot be pronounced. Beheld but not spoken. Some have seen this *Yod Hey Vav Hey* as a shortened form *Yahveh asher yehyeh,* "The One who brings into existence whatever exists."[9] With this One we do not talk. There is nothing to say. On an internal level one can bring together disparate elements of the psyche into an integrated self. (On the tree of the *sefirot,* this level is *tiferet,* or balance, the center in which everything is integrated. Indeed, the Name of Being is the trunk of the tree.)[10]

## The Name of Not-even-yet-Being

After Being is Becoming. Above the anthropomorphic God of this kingdom who permits description and relationship, above the One of Being whose Name cannot even be pronounced but whose Being can at least be fathomed, there is the One of Becoming who properly does not even yet have a Name.

Biblical Hebrew has only two tenses, usually called past and future, but more precisely perfect and imperfect. It understands actions as either completed or not completed. And it is in this "not yet" that God answers Moses at the bush. "Moses said to God, 'When I come to the people of Israel and say to them, 'The God of your parents has sent me to you," and they ask me, "What is the Name?" what shall I answer them?' And God said to Moses, *'Ehyeh asher Ehyeh' "* (Exod. 3:13–14). Not the "present" and static "I am that I am"; or even the dynamic future, "I will be who I will be"; but the yet imperfect, "I am not yet who I am not yet." God in effect says, "I am still Myself, becoming."

## The Name of the One

Still higher, according to some traditions, is the name of Unity itself. Not power or Being or even Becoming, but Oneness. The awesome consciousness that all power and being and Becoming are manifestations of a higher unity. *Hear O Israel,* listen to me, you who are locked in life and death struggling with the Nameless One, *The Lord your God*—the real name of the One you would serve and seek is, knowing that all *being is*—none other than, and only, *One* (Deut. 6:4). But it is a unity as yet unrealized—perhaps because we cannot keep it "conscious" long enough. If we could "pronounce" that unity—it would cease to be in the future. "On that day the Lord shall be One and his name shall be One" (Zech. 14:9).

## The Name of Nothing

But there is yet a higher Name for the One of Being, even as there is a higher evolutionary form of consciousness, and this is Nothing. Beyond One there is only Nothing, for only Nothing can comprehend both good and evil, being and becoming, unity and duality, sea and dry land. Already hinted at in Kabbalistic tradition by the ultimate Name, *Ayn Sof:* literally, without end or utter Nothingness. It is here that our consciousness and the Name of God while still discrete, are no longer separate. Here the primordial consciousness—light of creation, the self-reflection at Sinai, and passing through the sea on dry ground—exists as an ever-present and simultaneous possibility.

## THE PRISMS OF CONSCIOUSNESS

All the great stories are not only historical but personal as well. Occurring not only as an event in the past of the people but also always "able" to happen at any moment in each individual's life. They are like prisms through which consciousness may be refracted over and over again. Each time with renewed serendipity. We become conscious—not in the sense of remembering, but like what the psychoanalysts call insight and the mystics call enlightenment—in a different mode. It is the same us, the same world, but for a moment we see it anew.

Aware now, for instance, that we have been expelled from Eden, stung with the yearning to return again, crushed by our own and our world's brokenness. The world is not the way it is supposed to be. And it is somehow our fault. We are aware of some dim, lost unity with parents back in the kitchen or raking leaves or walking in the garden when things were whole and there was no thought or need to separate our selves from ourselves in order to see or understand or be conscious.

Or we become aware now that having once stood at the foot of the blazing mountain and beheld for just a moment the blinding light of the awareness of the Holy One of Being, that we are able to return to that place again and again. The promise of looking back into our own awareness is ever present. The Moses of the past and the Elijah of the future are both possible within us now. Consciousness beholds itself.

Or we become aware that the creation of light is likewise a perpetual possibility. Within us. This unintelligible movement surging through the cosmos and our very limbs is also the medium through which we write/read these words. Reminded every Sabbath that the work of creation is (can be) complete. A day that begins and ends with the flickering of a candle. The most important light is from the braided *Havdalla* candle lit just after the conclusion of Sabbath. As if to represent the first act of the work of creation begun anew. This light of *Havdalla* is none other than the light of our just created awareness, which must now be extinguished—as it were, like that ancient light of old—hidden away. But we remember what it looked like and are strengthened to make it through the week until we are again permitted to light the Sabbath candles.

There remains but one other prism. In the *Kiddush,* the prayer sanctifying the day, chanted just after the *Shabbos* candles are lit, there are allusions to creation and rest, and receiving the commandments of the Holy One. But there is also one phrase that at first seems curiously out of place. This day, it says, also commemorates our going forth from Egypt. To be sure, of all the myths, the great redemption needs no interpretation. The simple story itself, so probably an actual historical event, retains its power and function: you were slaves to Pharaoh, the king of permanence. Once you may have been free-as-the-wind nomads, but you wandered into that seductive, secure, unchanging Goshen and settled there. You stayed there so long you forgot even what it could mean to be free. (Neurosis invariably involves fear of some novelty.) And the One of Being brought you out from there, divided the sea so that you could cross on dry ground. In a theology of consciousness, there is yet another possible reading.

Ignore the specific references to places and people. Focus instead on the dynamic: once you were unable to be free, unable to even imagine novelty and spontaneity. Your life was a prison of once-perceived securities and defenses. And then the One of Being brought you to the edge of a "great sea" and you *passed through* the waters and you made it to the other side. There is in all this the unmistakable whisper of death, transformation, and rebirth. The great redemption does not come only at the end. For rebirth comes also at the beginning. A prism of consciousness, like the others, possible at any moment, through which our consciousness is exposed to itself as "having been a slave" and how itself goes through the waters, emerging on the other side a free being. Consciousness cannot be transformed and reborn until it is willing to walk through the water.


## THE GOING OUT FROM EGYPT

Reconsider the going out from Egypt. Not as an historical event or even a mythic one. But as the story of the transformation of consciousness. For above all we remember that at the beginning of the story there were slaves. And at the end of the story, when the children of Israel sang the Song at the Sea (Exod. 15), there were only free people. That in the service and by the strength of the One of Being this has (and continues to) come about: the transformation. That on account of this event the very structure of consciousness has been altered. The colored bits of light have been rearranged into a new pattern on the glass. Same glass. Same light. But the prism has caused something that has until this moment never been. There are at least four parts to the process; each one of which is recounted in the Exodus narrative.

On the tenth day of the month, the people are told to take to each one of their homes a lamb (Exod. 12 ff.). The spring lamb. The paschal offering. But, above all, a lamb that is also an Egyptian god.[11] In every household of slaves (who have so nearly assimilated the culture of the oppressor that they cannot even believe Moses when he comes to them), there is now even the god of Egypt itself. They must wonder as to the purpose of Moses and their ancient imageless god. They must wonder as they tie the lamb to their most permanent possession, their bed, why everyone must now own the local god. And what will they say to their Egyptian masters when they make inquiries? Does this mean the people of Israel have now become Egyptian? For four days it goes on. Long enough that it cannot be concealed. (The number of days between Yom Kippur—the day of Turning, and the beginning of Sukkot—the festival of wandering.) And then on the eve of the fourteenth day of the lunar month of spring (a full moon)—*Aviv-Nisan,* Moses tells them to slaughter the lamb-god. "And all the aggregate community of Israel shall slaughter it at twilight . . . and you shall take its blood and smear it on the door posts of your slave huts . . . (Exod. 6:7). Does God not know whose house belongs to whom!? No. It is not a sign for the One of Being, it is a sign for the slaves. It is a choice for them. An existential crisis. An unequivocal deed that may not be ignored, reconsidered, or postponed. The Egyptians know we own the god. They have seen

Come tomorrow and its blood is on our door, we leave with Moses, or they will surely kill us. A slave who can kill the master's god is no longer a slave. And if we are afraid to kill the lamb, then we may not leave with Moses. We may pretend we are still one of the people of Israel, but it will only be pretending. And this then is the first part of the transformation of consciousness. One must irrevocably choose to destroy the god of the oppressor, which you have taken into your home. It cannot be done in secret or post-pcned for even a day. You must stake your very life upon it. "You must not go outside your door until morning" (Exod. 12:22). Now it is in the hands of the One of Being. "I shall go through Egypt and execute judgment on all the gods of Egypt" (Exod. 12:12).

This is the second stage. That the One of Being would settle the score. "I personally and not an angel."[12] For once the alien god is destroyed, the forces of transformation are set into motion throughout the entire land. All during the night. You must remain in your hut. While other powers do their work. Layers of con-sciousness both within and beyond our psyche are now also freed to continue the work. There is a legend that even the king of Egypt himself, terrified that he might die, sought out Moses on that "watch night." But now he could not enter the slave hut. And we imagine that, come the next morning, there was not an Egyptian to be found. Streets deserted of masters. Open to free people. "And the children of Israel set out . . . six hundred thousand . . . a mixed multitude" (Exod. 12:37–38). Thinking they were free, at least until they arrived at the edge of the sea and saw Pharaoh and his chariots behind them.

This is the third stage. The story teaches that part of every experience of transformation involves a second confrontation. Even more frightening than before. The coming up once again of the enemy whom we were sure we had destroyed. The return of the repressed. Three steps forward, but two back. The Midrash suggests that there were four groups there at the edge of the sea. Each group, each part of us, received an answer according to its intention. Some of us wanted to throw ourselves into the sea but were told, "Have no fear! Stand by and witness the deliverance which the Lord will work for you today" (Exod. 14:13). Others chose to surrender and return to the slave pits, but were assured, "The Egyptians whom you see today you will never see again" (Exod. 14:13). Still others wanted to stand and do battle. They were calmed with the promise, "The Lord will battle for you" (Exod. 14:14). And the last group, who simply raised their voices in prayer, were silenced. "Hold your peace!" (Exod. 14:14). Only one of the six hundred thousand, Naḥshon ben Aminadav, walked forward into what was to become a path through the waters, and for him alone and the rest of us by the merit of his singleness of purpose, was the sea split.[13] Perhaps one of the most insightful descriptions of existential panic recorded. Here, at the edge, with the enemy, who is also of us, rising up again to destroy us.

Once, in a workshop, we acted out this scene at the sea. Members of the group each being one of the story's rubrics. Someone was the sea and someone else Moses and so forth. The person who played "god" stood on a chair and watched. Pharaoh coming closer. The people's panic. The sea's refusal. Moses' bewilderment. And all of us, we who knew what was "supposed" to happen (everyone knows the story), began to feel an uneasiness as "god" refused to "split" the sea. We all agreed that "god" had but this one thing to do and felt a genuine fear that in this reenactment, this "god" might let "playing god" go to his head and remain silent! People actually said to god, "C'mon god, split the sea!" The anxiety grew greater still, until it seemed as though our dream-play would end in nightmare disaster. And then, at the last possible emotional moment, "god," in almost a whisper, said only, "It's time now." People actually cheered. The sea almost with gratitude acknowledged a power greater than its own and rolled aside. And the children of Israel went through its midst on dry ground. And it occurred to us, in retrospect, that this is perhaps all the One of

Being ever says: "It's time now." You may enter "the waters" and not be destroyed. Only transformed. The very waters that will purify you will at the same time rid you forever of (a part of you named) Pharaoh and his soldiers.

And this is the final stage. The passing through the waters. Like Jacob, our father, before us, who as the final act of return to his brother Esau, chose to be alone, by the edge of the waters of the river Jabok (which probably served as the boundary of the Land of Israel), and who wrestled there with the angel-person until the breaking of dawn and who, on account of his survival, was granted the name Israel, thus the children of Israel, and we, their grand-children, are permitted to pass through the water and become new beings. For this reason, all acts of personal purification and conversion in traditional Judaism require immersion in the *mikveh,* the ritual bath. Completely naked, we come up out of the water new beings. Having destroyed the enemy's god. Remained inside during the watch night. Endured the return of the oppressor and at last passing through the waters. Death. Transformation. Rebirth. *Baruch ata Adonai,* Holy One of blessing, *M'chayeh Ha'Maytim,* the One who resurrects the dead.[14]

What drowns in the Red Sea is not Pharaoh and his armies, but an aspect of the ego. It is reabsorbed into the personality, but forever gone as a dynamic force. And so likewise this "passing through the waters" "from slavery into freedom" is a prophecy of what will in the future happen to all being. In the days of the anointed One.

## TESHUVA: THE RETURNING TO NOTHING

Before the world was created, the Holy One, blessed be He, with his Name alone existed. And He got the idea to create the world. So He began to trace the foundations of being before Him. But it would not stand. Not until He also created a way for it to return to the Nothingness from whence it began. A means for coming back. Repentance. Dying. *Teshuva.* [15]

*Teshuva,* you must understand, is not so much an act of individual repentence, as customarily rendered, or apology, or even (re)-turning into the self and telling the truth. It is a movement of return on a cosmic scale. It is the second half of one great universal rhythm, which those who "make *Teshuva*" enter. For when they do, they find themselves therein joined with countless others who are also finding their way home. "Through *Teshuva* all things are reunited with God."[16] One who enters this hidden, pulsing returning to the source is ultimately renewed. Transformed. Reborn. In the words of Rav Kook, "In the great channel in which the life sustaining force flows, there is revealed the unitary source of all existence, and in the hovering, life-serving spirit of *Teshuva* all things are renewed to a higher level. . . ."[17] The creation and maintenance of being require a kind of rhythmic moving out from and a returning to the point of beginning. The Nothing that precedes the something of Being. To remain aware of this movement is the underlying purpose of all the rituals and rehearsals of sacred truth. It is the very breathing out and breathing in of the universe itself. Breathing out must follow breathing in even as it is the prerequisite for the next breathing out.

According to the work of Russian meteorologist-mathematician Alexander Friedman, if matter in the universe is above a certain average density, then the resultant gravitational field will curve the lines of expansion back in upon themselves and the cosmos itself will return to the point from whence it began. Spiritual traditions are able to be much more daring and have for centuries spoken of cosmic cycles of expansion and contraction, or *Shmetot.* God, they whisper, made and unmade other universes before this one. Now of course this can only be a matter of cosmologic theory. And whether our universe will continue to expand into a frozen emptiness or return into an ever-contracting fireball is still a subject of debate among scientists. But its "return" is a very reasonable possibility.

This life-death rhythm is an apparent necessity for the perpetuation of the species through genetic means. Procreation and disintegration are not opposing forces but both dimensions of a greater One. "In biological fact . . . sex and death are causally linked. Nature sees to it that any species which reproduces the genes by sexual union of two individuals has built in mechanisms which ensure the elimination of the parents so as to allow space for the new genetic material to grow and to reproduce in its turn. In other words, death is essential to genetic diversification through sexual union."[18] Parents must die in order for children to live. "Only birth can conquer death—the birth, not of the old thing again, but of something new. Within the soul, within the body social, there must be—if we are to experience long survival—a continuous 'recurrence of birth' to nullify the unremitting recurrences of death."[19] Of the slaves who left Egypt (with the exception of only two, and they are literally another story), all that generation died in the wilderness. It is a bittersweet truth, this breathing out and breathing in. But we acknowledge and understand it. Even as we stake our lives and the lives of our children on it. Like fallen leaves enriching the soil, it is true. This return of the genes and the generations must occur if new ones are to set out.

Even a beam of light moving at the maximum allowable speed of the universe (the speed of light) somehow does not move in a straight line. Its packets of photons move up and then down in the manner of a wave. Pulsing, oscillating waves of massless subatomic particles permeate not only all light but all being as well. Never still, they perpetually move out and return. It is the same with generations of creatures, galaxies, and ordinary human beings who on occasion are moved to draw back from a hurtful stance and say, "I am sorry."

Each apology must involve this retreat from some territory thought conquered by the self. Only now we understand that it did not belong to us and never did. And we "return" to our place.

Diminish the size of our ego. Become as Nothing. Such Nothingness is not a denial but a return to our source. "In Hasidic thought this . . . is called *Ayin*, 'Nothingness,' because of this stage of the divine process nothing can be said; it is utterly beyond all human comprehension. When a man attains to the stage of self-annihilation he can thus be said to have reached the world of the divine Nothingness. Emptied of selfhood his soul has now become attached to the true reality, the divine Nothingness."[20]

Such self-emptying is also referred to as *Bitul Ha'Yesh*, making substance nothing. And the letters for the pronoun "I" (in Hebrew, *Ani, alef nun yod*) can be rearranged *alef yod nun* so as to make the word *Ayin* or "Nothingness" (ego death). Thus the self is transformed from the "substance" of ego to the Nothingness that preceeds all (new) creation and is intimately connected to the highest orders of the Holy One of Being, also called the *Ayn Sof*, the One of no end.

When we perform *Teshuva*, we thus fall back into the source of our being. We reexperience the Nothingness whence we have come. When consciousness is able to attain such a level it is like light being pulled back into a black hole in space. Into an Einsteinian "singularity." When the "mass" of the galaxy or the ego exceeds a critical density it collapses back into itself. The necessary prelude to any rebirth.

Each act of repentance also confesses our ultimate mortality. It is the rehearsal for a death that will punctuate the end of this life's awareness. Just as the death of each creature is in turn a rehearsal for the death of a species and a galaxy and a cosmos. The great rhythm of going out and returning. Now this kind of death is not an end but only the beginning of a transformation that will generate a rebirth. You cannot be reborn until you are willing to die. The night of liberation from Egypt was also a night of dying. The lamb. The first born. The destroyer. The slaves. Blood on the doorposts.

The great day of communal atonement/repentence/*Teshuva* in Judaism, Yom Kippur, is likewise intimately associated with death. We do not eat or drink or perfume ourselves or have sex. We dress in white (shrouds). There is one return after another. The liturgy is all of returning. In other words, we rehearse our own death. Whenever you perform *Teshuva* you die a little, fall back into your source and forward into your destiny. But it is not a painful death. As so many reports of those who have actually come close now suggest, there is peace and light. The dying returns to the Nothing and the rebirth comes from out of it. Rising up from the primeval ocean. At first on fins, then on legs, at last by wings. Then they come too close to the sun and begin the inescapable spiral back into the abyss. But from that emptiness they are transformed. A new generation is regenerated and rises up.

When I began it was from Nothing. The source of all creation is Nothing. When I die I shall return to this Nothing. And when I am reborn it will be from out of this same Nothing. *Barukh ata Adonai,* Holy One of blessing, *M'chayeh Ha'Matim,* the One who resurrects the dead.[21]

Look who I was yesterday, last year, as a child, in my last life! But that one is no more and yet I live on! Is this not perhaps the reason the legend tells that we do not see Adam until we die? Perhaps the Adam spoken of is not the first Adam of the Garden but the primordial Adam. The one who precedes all creation. The one whose form abides within the Nothingness.


## THE ATONEMENT


There is a story told of Rabbi Elimelekh of Lizhensk.[22] There once came before the Rabbi a man whose life, having been marked with many sins, wished to make repentance. He sought direction in ordering whatever acts might be necessary for a complete return. Rabbi Elimelekh consented and told the man that first he would have to liquidate all his assets. The furniture, the jewelry, the real estate, the inheritance. And with everything thus converted into cash he was to come back. Only then would the Rabbi help him to make repentance. The man did so and stood now with everything he owned as a pile of money on the table in front of the sage. It was a great liquid fortune. The bills were paid. The last links severed. "Now we are ready to begin to order the repentance. Write for us," asked Elimelekh, "all your sins and evil doings and transgressions on a sheet of paper and give it to me." Again, the man did as he was told and Elimelekh then began to read the confession aloud. The man was overcome by the weight of his own shame and guilt but the Rabbi read on. After a short time even the Rabbi seemed shocked by the enormity of the sins and himself cried out in pain. "How could one do such things!?" The man swooned and fell to the floor unconscious. But Elimelekh revived him and went on with the reading. Again the sage cried out in astonishment and again the man collapsed at the recounting of his own wickedness, only to be reawakened by the sage. This crying out in disbelief and fainting and reviving went on seven times during the reading of the list. When at last the ordeal was completed, Rabbi Elimelekh shook his head. "For sins as grave as these there can be but one atonement: death. Such would have been the verdict of the High Court when the Temple still stood. The means for such an execution are burning." And the Rabbi then explained how such a capital punishment was to be carried out according to ancient legal tradition. They would take molten lead and pour it down the throat, thus burning the condemned man from the inside. But even when the man heard this, his desire to make repentance was so great that he willingly accepted the verdict and with trembling, the punishment. "I will do whatever must be done."

He took a few coins from the pile of money before him and bought a metal spoon, some tin (for the flux), and some lead. He then returned to the Rabbi's house. There Elimelekh told him to make the fire and melt the tin and the lead in the spoon, being careful to see to it that they were properly mixed. The man did all this with complete devotion. And when he reported the smelting done, the Rabbi asked him to lay himself on the floor and put on a blindfold. Rabbi Elimelekh then had him recite the final confession which the man did with a broken heart and great trembling. He took upon himself full responsibility for his sins and their punishment. He recited the six words of the *Shema,* the declaration of God's unity. "Now open your mouth so that I may pour the molten lead down your throat. . . . " At that instant, the Rabbi took instead a spoonful of marmalade and put it in the man's open mouth. "You have made full atonement. Now get up, stand on your feet, serve the One whose Name is blessed, for you are another being. Take this money on the table and use it as a righteous man. . . ."

Consciousness dies not when we die, but once we are willing to enter the Nothingness. Rabbi Dov Baer of Mezritch taught that "a person needs to regard [himself] as if [he] were nothing. Forget yourself in every way. . . . Only then will you be able to attain ultimate preparation, which is the same as the world of consciousness, for there, everything is equal, Life and death, sea and dry land. . . ."[23]

Only after Abraham is able to say, "I too want to be buried here," does he emerge from the cave. Only once Abraham is willing to concede his own mortality is he able to return to life.

# Chapter 7

# Living in the River

*If . . . consciousness ceases to ignore itself and becomes fully self-conscious, it discovers . . . that there is no little man inside, no "I" who owns this consciousness. And if that is so, if I do not own my consciousness, and if there is even no "me" to own it, to receive it, or to put up with it, who on earth is there to be either the victim of fate or the master of nature? "What is troubling us," said Wittgenstein, "is the tendency to believe that the mind is like a little man within."*
—*Alan Watts* [1]

*We have acquired a true knowledge of God. . . . [When] speaking with others, or attending to our bodily wants, our mind is all that time with God; when we are with our heart constantly near God, even whilst our body is in the society of men. . .*

*Moses Maimonides* [2]

*The Abraham story, of course, has no
end. It had no beginning. It existed for only the momentary space between going
to the herd to get a calf and returning. For this reason, this last chapter can only
continue on with the biblical text: Having lunch with three strangers. . . .*

*"Abraham! Abraham! . . . Do you hear me? Are you all right? Do you have
the calf? Here are the curds you asked me to prepare. Where have you been? Help
me now. We have guests. . . ." says Sarah.*

*"I hear you, my dove," Abraham answers. "Here is the calf. What needs to
be done? . . . But don't let me forget, after they've gone, I have a story for you,
you won't believe . . . "*

*She smiles. (She already knows the story.) They serve the lunch.*

But there is something even beyond Nothingness. You see, this
journey does not end in Eden. Its fulfillment does not coincide
with paradise, but with our return from it. Abraham returns home
for lunch. He reenters the narrative of his life. It is not that he
abandons the Garden; for him, the father of Jewish spirituality, the
ultimate achievement is always to return to this world and this life

and this moment. And, above all, to be with the people he momentarily left behind.

I am sitting in the study. Reading. Listening to music. Thinking. Or simply looking out the window and one of the children calls. "Daddy, do this for me." "Daddy, my brother hit me." "Daddy, listen to this." It is all the same. Now, I ask you, who is to say that their summons is not, finally, more important than the Garden, with its tree in the center, and the four rivers?

A physicist once patiently cautioned me, after I had just begun to learn of the preposterous possibilities that particle physics suggests—how time and space can be bent and how particles can move through matter and so forth—that while it was all true, I had, just to play it safe, best not try walking through plate glass windows. In the final analysis, for all our fantastic journeys, there remains this world to receive us. And, for this reason, any "spirituality" that claims to forever transcend, escape, or otherwise transgress this everyday world, is a fraud. There are four people waiting back at the tent for lunch.

Judaism has many legends of people who go on spiritual journeys. Who through accident or by design are blessed or cursed to look upon the Garden. And all of the stories, in one way or another, have a surprising conclusion. The visitor is given a choice. The searcher who has just arrived is rewarded with the final question: "And now that you have survived and beheld these wonders, do you choose to remain here with 'us' or will you return to your spouse and children?" Whereupon, the visitor is invariably devastated. "Oh my God! I forgot all about them! They must be worried sick! Are they all right?" So you must make a choice. Which will it be: Those ordinary people who did not understand and perhaps may never understand, yet by whose nurture and struggle you have lived to attain this blessed moment; or worldless bliss here with spiritual beings who are beyond such humanity? And here is the twist.

If the searcher chooses to remain with eternity, the searcher loses eternity! If the searcher chooses this finite world, the searcher is rewarded with eternity! This is expressed in a slightly different way by the saying that the pious are not in paradise, paradise is in the pious.[3] We do not know if the question was ever put to Abraham. We are told only that he returned to lunch.

## WITH MIRRORS FOR EYES

Rabbi Naḥman of Bratslav explained the verse "Face to face the Lord spoke to you" (Deut. 5:4), "When they received the Torah, Israel had a shining (mirror-like) countenance, and were thus able to receive the holy face, so that this holy face would be visible in them. . . ."[4] At the moment of revelation, the One is seen in the face of the other. Psychoanalysis and spiritual search are alike in this respect. For both there is a looking back into one's own eyes in such a way that one looks out through them again as if with new eyes.

It is, of course, a risky business. (Even the description turns to air in the face of sustained logical inquiry.) An error could result in madness ("I am god!") or an equally damaging cynicism ("There is no god!"). One must have a teacher. A guide. A therapist. For God's sake at least a *ḥaver*—a holy partner. Who has been there. Inside out and back again.

This is a search with an unattainable goal. It has many names. Enlightenment. Wisdom. Wholeness. Fulfillment. Vision. Peace. *Devekut,* being at one with. But all share this strange process of once having returned deep into oneself—or the Self—and survived. And returned with eyes remade for wonder. Here is the sequence; it corresponds to the names of God.

### 1. *Ani:* I

On the first level, there is only consciousness. Person who is alive and eating. Corresponding to *Ani,* "I." No god. Autism. To such a person apply the words "One who is full of oneself has no room for god."

### 2. *Elohim:* god; *Shaddai:* power

Then there is becoming aware of oneself in contradistinction to other selves. There are powers in the universe other and sometimes greater than my own. There are people around us who define our childhoods. This is also the god called *Shaddai* or *Elohim.* A strange kind of limiting that is the touchstone for all religion. And while it often seems to cripple, devastate, or frighten—creating a consciousness that is closed off, obeisant, broken, rebellious—it usually initiates a sense of awe, wonder, and mystery. The beginning of search. Beginning of therapy. There is someone more than me here.

### 3. *YHWH: Adonai:* The Lord of Being

Now on a higher level is the realization of one's own consciousness. Sense of self. The Lord *Yod Hey Vav Hey.* The one of Being. The therapist, teacher, friend holds up a mirror and we behold who we are. Neither all the universe like child, nor frightened and anxious on account of it, but one human being within it. One human being with other beings.

### 4. *Ehyeh:* I am not yet

Above this level no one may ascend by will or perseverance alone. A gift from above, an undeserved favor must be granted. Here at last is the ability to imagine that we might become other than we now are. *Ehyeh asher Ehyeh:* I am not yet. This is done from within when we (the students) discover that the next thing to do, after studying the reply of the teacher (whose silence shows us who we are), is to find within ourselves our own mirrors. One mirror "looking" at another mirror.

### 5. *Echad:* One

There is no longer confusion. While the reciprocated images are the same on each "glass," each side, each discrete mirror is precious and indispensable. This is the meaning of *Echad* unity. That the image on the mirrors is the same even though each mirror remains unique unto itself. "Hear O Israel, the Lord our God, the Lord is One" (Deut. 6:4).

### 6. *Ayin:* Nothingness

Until at last, in giving up the struggle for individuality, we know that our unique gifts cannot be withheld. Now there can be *Ayin.* Nothingness. For the Lord of this consciousness is the *Ayn Sof,* the One without end. The apparent world of differences, fallen away, gives way to a return to a self no longer at odds with brothers and sisters or its infinite source. The ultimate self-reference loop. The eye beholds itself. No more silver on the back of the mirror—only glass.[5] The one who set out in search of a distant mountain has found, on the way, that he is the mountain. And Moses gazed over the whole land. No longer any difference between fantasy and life. Repression melts. Something logically impossible, unthinkable indeed, something truly messianic happens. The river of light now flows upon the surface of the land.

### 7. *Ani:* I

As the three letters of the Hebrew word *Ayin—Ayin, Yod, Nun:* "Nothingness"—rearrange themselves again (and again) into the primary *Ani, Ayin, Nun, Yod,* "I," and I who was nothing return again (and again) to I who am only I. It has been "I" all along. The one reading/writing these words. Caught up in the net of using, selling, working, forgetting is the One. Is this not the great mystery of religious consciousness? That the one who began as the fool has ascended through the heights of heaven. Through all the rungs of consciousness and divinity. Back to this ordinary person who feels somehow blessed to simply awaken each morning. What loftier goal could there be for any therapy? (All we can do, warned Freud, is transform your hysterical misery into common unhappiness.)[6] The "I" that set out is different from the very same "I" that has returned. What seems to be a perfect circle, upon a change of vantage, is revealed now to have been a spiral.

And what other goal for religion could there be? To see the Holy Ancient One face to face. Or through Scripture to reimagine the story and thus be reminded of its ever-present possibility. Or through ritual, whose sacred script compels us to act as if we were dreaming, to relive it.

Go on. Bring the dream into waking. Join each one of its discrete words into one long name of God. Endure the silence in which it is heard, there at the foot of the mountain. Feel that subtle consciousness form the very protoplasm of our collective body. Return through that body to the light of creation itself. Allow that light to dissolve the "letters" of ego into Nothing. And be reborn.

See once again, gently pulsing beneath all being, a river of light. Permit it to rise to the surface. Realize that the one gazing at the river and the river are one. We are the light.

# Epilogue

"And Abraham passed away; he died at a good ripe age, old and full; and he was gathered to his people. His sons, Isaac and Ishmael, buried him in the cave of Machpelah. . . . "
—Genesis 25:8–9

# Notes

## LEGEND OF ABRAHAM'S JOURNEY

1. All talmudic references in these notes are to the Babylonian Talmud.
2. *Zohar* I 127b.
3. *Zohar* I 127a; see also *Pirke de Rabbi Eliezer* 36 (Midrash).
4. *Zohar* II 210b.
5. *Zohar* I 128a.
6. *Zohar* I 57b.
7. *Zohar* I 128a.
8. *Tanḥuma, Lekh Lekha* 9 (Midrash).

## CHAPTER 1: LIKE ONES IN A DREAM

1. Owen Barfield, "Dream, Myth and Philosophical Double Vision," in *Myths, Dreams and Religion,* ed. Joseph Campbell (New York: Dutton, 1970), p. 216.
2. Herbert Fingarette, *The Self in Transformation: Psychoanalysis, Philosophy and the Life of the Spirit* (New York: Harper & Row, Harper Torchbooks, 1965), p. 175.
3. *Berachot* 56a (Talmud).
4. *Gen. Rabba* 1.1 (Midrash).
5. Much of the remainder of this chapter was originally delivered as a lecture entitled "Hayinu K'Holmim: An Alternative Metaphor for the Teaching of Torah," at the Annual Convention of the Central Conference of American Rabbis in Toronto, 1978, and appears in their yearbook.
6. Cf. Lyall Watson, *Lifetide: The Biology of the Unconcious* (New York: Bantam Books, 1980), pp. 205, 211.
7. Norman O. Brown, *Life Against Death: The Psycho-analytic Meaning of History* (Middletown, Conn.: Wesleyan University Press, 1959), p. 319.
8. Cf. C. G. Jung, "The Concept of the Collective Unconcious," in *The Portable Jung,* trans. R. F. C. Hull, ed. Joseph Campbell (New York: Viking, 1971), pp. 60, 66.
9. Johannes Pedersen, *Israel: Its Life and Culture,* vol. I (London: Oxford University Press, 1926), p. 135.
10. Cf. Joseph Campbell, *The Hero with a Thousand Faces* (Princeton, N.J.: Princeton University Press, 1949), p. 19.

11. Cf. C. G. Jung, *Psychology and Religion* (New Haven, Conn.: Yale University Press, 1938), p. 45.
12. Emil A Gutheil, *The Handbook of Dream Analysis* (New York: Liveright, 1951), p. 550.
13. *Pesachim* 7b (Talmud).
14. Emil Gutheil, *Handbook,* p. 41.
15. *Baba Metzia* 86b (Talmud).
16. *Baba Metzia* 86b–87a (Talmud).
17. Erich Fromm, The Forgotten Language (New York: Grove Press, 1951), pp. 215–216.
18. *Zohar* I 127a.
19. Johannes Pedersen, *Israel,* p. 136.
20. Cf. Sigmund Freud, "Moral Responsibility for Dreams," in Herbert Fingarette, *The Self in Transformation,* p. 196.
21. Norman O. Brown, *Life Against Death,* pp. 320–321.
22. Frederick S. Perls, "Dream Seminars," in *Gestalt Therapy Now,* ed. Joen Fagan and Irma Lee Shepherd (New York: Harper & Row, 1971), p. 212.
23. Erich Neumann, *The Origins and History of Consciousness* (Princeton, N.J.: Princeton University Press, 1954), p. 276.
24. Ira Progoff, "Waking Dream and Living Myth," in Campbell, *Myth, Dreams and Religion,* pp. 176–177.
25. Herbert Fingarette, *The Self in Transformation,* p. 176.
26. *Sota* 34a (Talmud).
27. Joseph Campbell, *The Masks of God: Occidental Mythology* (New York: Viking, 1964), pp. 519–521.
28. Sigmund Freud, "Moral Responsibility," in Fingarette, *The Self in Transformation,* p. 180.
29. Cf. *Zohar* III 152a.
30. *Berachot* 55b (Talmud).

## CHAPTER 2: THE RIVER OF LIGHT

1. Aldous Huxley, *The Doors of Perception* (New York: Harper & Row, Perennial Library, 1970), pp. 22–23, citing C. D. Broad and Henri Bergson.
2. *Zohar* III 58a.
3. Aldous Huxley, *Doors,* p. 22.
4. *Gen. Rabba* 56.1–2 (Midrash).
5. Huston Smith, *Forgotten Truth: The Primordial Tradition* (New York: Harper & Row, 1976), p. 62.
6. *Berachot* 10a (Talmud).
7. Rabbi Dov Baer of Mezritch, *Maggid Devarav Leyakov,* ed. Rivka Schatz-Uffenheimer (Jerusalem: Magnes Press, 1976), p. 186, no. 110.

8. Erich Neumann, *The Origins and History of Conciousness* (Princeton, N.J.: Princeton University Press, 1954), p. 275.

9. *Berachot* 2a (Talmud).

10. Cf. Paul Watzlawick, *The Language of Change: Elements of Therapeutic Communication* (New York: Basic Books, 1978), ch. 6.

11. *Sabbath and Festival Prayer Book (Vetaher Libenu)* (Sudbury, Mass: Congregation Beth El of the Sudbury River Valley, 1980), pp. 6 ff.

12. *Pirke Avot* 5.22 (Talmud).

13. Herbert Fingarette, *The Self in Transformation: Psychoanalysis, Philosophy and the Life of the Spirit* (New York: Harper & Row, Harper Torchbooks, 1965), p. 33.

14. *Tanḥuma, Pekuday* 3 (Midrash); see also Adolph Jellinek, ed., *Beit HaMidrash,* vol. I (Jerusalem: Wahrmann Books, 1967), pp. 153–158.

15. Loren Eiseley, *The Immense Journey* (New York: Random House, Vintage, 1957), p. 125.

16. Sigmund Freud, *A General Introduction to Psychoanalysis,* trans. Joan Riviere (Garden City, N.Y.: Doubleday, 1943), lecture 19.

17. Huston Smith, *Forgotten Truth.*

18. Julian Jaynes, *The Origin of Consciousness in the Breakdown of the Bicameral Mind* (Boston: Houghton Mifflin, 1976).

19. *Tanḥuma, Pekuday* 3 (Midrash); see also Jellinek, *Beit HaMidrash,* pp. 153–158.

20. *Zohar* III 61b.

21. *Avot de Rabbi Natan 31* (Talmud); see also *Zohar* I 90a–91b.

22. Richard L. Rubenstein, *The Religious Imagination: A Study in Psychoanalysis and Jewish Tehology* (Indianopolis, Ind.: Bobbs-Merrill, 1968), p. 55.

23. Erwin Singer, *Key Concepts in Psychotherapy,* 2d ed. (New York: Basic Books, 1970), p. 71.

24. Ibid., p. 69.

25. Lyall Watson, *Lifetide: The Biology of the Unconcious* (New York: Bantam, 1980), p. 153.

26. Loren Eiseley, *The Immense Journey,* p. 109.

## CHAPTER 3: THE SELF-REFLECTION AT SINAI

1. Paul Watzlawick, *The Language of Change: Elements of Therapeutic Communication* (New York: Basic Books, 1978), p. 96.

2. Rabbi Kalynomos of Kalmish (Shapiro) of Pieasetsna, *Aysh Kodesh (Holy Fire)* (Jerusalem, 1960), p. 150.

3. Loren Eiseley, *The Immense Journey* (New York: Random House, Vintage, 1957), pp. 120–121.

4. Erich Neumann, *The Origins and History of Conciousness* (Princeton, N.J.: Princeton University Press, 1954), p. 6, quoting Ernst Cassirer.

5. Cf. *Song of Songs Rabba* 5.16.3 (Midrash); *Exod. Rabba* 29.4 (Midrash); and *Shabbat* 88b (Talmud).

6. Ibid.

7. *Berachot* 8b (Talmud).

8. Cf. Joel Kovel, *White Rascism: A Psychohistory* (New York: Random House, Vintage, 1970), ch. 7 and Appendix.

9. *Mekhilta de Rabbi Ishmael, BaHodesh (Yitro)* 9 (Midrash).

10. *Exod. Rabba* 5.9 (Midrash).

11. Ibid.

12. Ibid.

13. Gershom Scholem, *On the Kabbalah and its Symbolism,* trans. Ralph Manheim (New York: Schocken, 1965), p. 65.

14. Louis Ginzberg, *The Legends of the Jews,* vol. VI (Philadelphia: The Jewish Publication Society, 1928), p. 45, note 243.

15. Gershom Scholem, *On the Kabbalah,* p. 30; see also *Exod. Rabba* 29.9 (Midrash).

16. Gershom Scholem, *The Messianic Idea in Judaism: And Other Essays on Jewish Spirituality* (New York: Schocken, 1971), p. 239.

17. *Pesikta Rabbatai* 4.2 (Midrash); see also *Zohar* I 208a ff.

18. *Pesachim* 54a (Talmud).

19. Lawrence Kushner, *Honey from the Rock: Visions of Jewish Mystical Renewal* (New York: Harper & Row, 1977), pp. 94. ff.

20. *Zohar* I 209a.

21. Gershom Scholem, "The Impact of Mysticism on Society: A Creative Paradox," paper delivered at the Conference on Mysticism and Society presented by the Frank L. Weil Institute for Studies in Religion and Humanities, Cincinnati, Ohio, April 16–18, 1966, p. 16.

22. Ibid., p. 18.

23. Ibid.

24. Lyall Watson, *Lifetide: The Biology of the Unconcious* (New York; Bantam, 1980), p. 50.

25. Ibid., p. 93.

26. Lewis Thomas, *The Lives of a Cell: Notes of a Biology Watcher* (New York: Bantam Books, 1975), p. 2.

27. Ibid.

28. Cf. Itzhak Bentov, *Stalking the Wild Pendulum: On the Mechanics of Consciousness* (New York: Dutton, 1977), pp. 58–62.

29. *Mekhilta de Rabbi Ishmael, Shirta (Beshalah)* 3 (Midrash).

30. *Exod. Rabba* 24.1 (Midrash).

31. *Zohar* II 82a.

32. *Exod. Rabba* 5.9 (Midrash).

33. Arthur Green, *Tormented Master: A Life of Rabbi Nahman of Bratslav* (University, Ala.: University of Alabama, 1979), p. 107, quoting Rabbi Nahman of Bratslav, *Likkutim* 22:10.

34. Martin Buber, *Tales of the Hasidim: The Early Masters,* trans. Olga Marx (New York: Schocken, 1947), p. 107.

35. *Birkat Ha-Hammah: A Liturgy for the Sun Cycle Blessing,* trans. Nehemia Polen and Lauri Wolff-Polen (11 Alpine Road, Everett, Mass., 1980), unpaged introduction.

36. *Exod. Rabba* 29.9 (Midrash).

37. Emil Fackenheim, *Quest for Past and Future* (Bloomington, Ind.: Indiana University Press, 1968), pp. 66 ff.

38. Burt Jacobson, "The Glorious Presence: An Interpretation of the Teachings of Rabbi Israel Baal Shem Tov," 2d draft (1978), p. 14.

## CHAPTER 4: PROTOPLASM OF CONCIOUSNESS

1. Gershom Scholem, *On the Kabbalah and Its Symbolism* (New York: Schocken, 1965), p. 115.

2. Norman O. Brown, *Love's Body* (New York: Random House, Vintage, 1966), p. 154.

3. John Archibald Wheeler, "The Universe as Home for Man," in *The American Scientist* 62 (Nov.–Dec. 1974): 689.

4. *Tanhuma, Pekuday* 6 (Midrash).

5. *Midrash Tehillim* 139.5 (Midrash); *Gen. Rabba* 7.1 (Midrash); *Lev. Rabba* 14.1 (Midrash); and *Berachot* 60a (Talmud).

6. Gershom Scholem, *On the Kabbalah,* p. 119.

7. *Hagigah* 12a (Talmud).

8. Louis Ginzberg, *The Legends of the Jews,* vol. I (Philadelphia: The Jewish Publication Society, 1928), p. 59; see also Louis Ginzberg, *Legends,* vol. V, p. 79, note 22.

9. Ibid., vol. I, p. 60.

10. Ibid., vol. V, p. 75, notes 19, 20 and pp. 112–113, note 104; *Tanhuma, Pekuday* 3, *Ki Tisa* 12 (Midrash); *Gen. Rabba* 8.1, 14.9 (Midrash); and *Song of Songs Rabba* 40.3 (Midrash).

11. Cf. Lewis Thomas, *The Lives of a Cell: Notes of a Biology Watcher* (New York: Bantam Books, 1975), ch. 1.

12. Cf. *Zohar* I 121b.

13. Cf. Norman O. Brown, *Life Against Death: The Psychoanalytic Meaning of History* (Middletown, Conn.: Wesleyan University Press, 1959), pp. 310–313.

14. William Irwin Thompson, *Darkness and Scattered Light: Speculation on the Future* (New York: Doubleday, Anchor, 1978), pp. 136–137, quoting the "Gaia Hypothesis" of Lovelock and Margolis.

15. Lewis Thomas, *Lives of a Cell,* p. 170.

16. Moses Maimonides, *Guide for the Perplexed,* trans. M. Friedlander (New York: Dover Publications, 1956), vol. I, ch. 72, p. 113.

17. Norman O. Brown, *Love's Body,* p. 152.

18. Alan W. Watts, *The Book: On the Taboo Against Knowing Who You Are* (New York: Macmillan Co., Collier, 1966), p. 6.

19. Cf. *Avot de Rabbi Natan* 31 (Talmud); *Berachot* 10a (Talmud).

20. Elaine Pagels, "The Discovery of the Gnostic Gospels," in *New York Review of Books* (Oct. 25, 1969): p. 33.

21. Burt Jacobson, "The Glorious Presence: An Interpretation of the Teachings of Rabbi Israel Baal Shem Tov," 2d draft (1978), p. 25.

22. Gershom Scholem, "The Impact of Mysticism on Society: A Creative Paradox," paper delivered at the Conference on Mysticism and Society presented by the Frank L. Weil Institute for Studies in Religion and Humanities, Cincinnati, Ohio, April 16–18, 1966, p. 24.

23. *Gen. Rabba* 8.10 (Midrash).

24. *Zohar* I 90b–91a; *Zohar* II 70a.

25. *Avot de Rabbi Natan* 31 (Talmud).

26. *Zohar* I 91a.

27. *Brain/Mind Bulletin* 5, no. 10 (April 7, 1980).

28. Paddy Chayevsky, *Altered States* (New York: Harper & Row, 1978).

29. Lyall Watson, *Lifetide: The Biology of the Unconcious* (New York: Bantam Books, 1980), p. 158.

30. *Brain/Mind Bulletin* 5, no. 19 (Aug. 18, 1980).

31. Lyall Watson, *Lifetide,* p. 164.

32. Ibid., pp. 40, 103.

33. S. E. Luria, *Life: The Unfinished Experiment* (New York: Scribners, 1973), p. 100.

34. Martin Buber, *I and Thou,* trans. Walter Kaufman (New York: Scribners, 1970), pp. 57–59.

35. David R. Blumenthal, *Understanding Jewish Mysticism: A Source Reader* (New York: Kitav, 1978), p. 141.

36. William Irwin Thompson, *Darkness and Scattered Light,* p. 20.

37. Lyall Watson, *Lifetide,* pp. 19, 377.

## CHAPTER 5: THE LIGHT OF CREATION

1. *Zohar* I 31b.

2. Eric Neumann, *The Origins and History of Conciousness* (Princeton, N.J.: Princeton University Press, 1954), p. 275.

3. Jacob Needleman, *A Sense of the Cosmos: The Encounter of Modern Science and Ancient Truth* (New York: Doubleday, 1975), p. 98.

4. *Gen. Rabba* 3.6 (Midrash).

5. Cf. Eliyahu Ki Tov, *Sefer Ha-Parshiyot, Parashat Vayikra* (Jerusalem: "A" Publishers, 1969), p. 11; also see *Zohar* I 31b.

6. *Avoda Zara* 8a (Talmud); *Avot de Rabbi Natan* 1 (Talmud).

7. Huston Smith, *Forgotten Truth: The Primordial Tradition* (New York: Harper & Row, 1976).

8. *Gen. Rabba* 1.1 (Midrash).

9. Gershom Scholem, *Zohar: The Book of Splendor,* trans. Gershom Scholem (New York: Schocken, 1949), pp. 27–28, *Zohar* I 15a.

10. Steven Weinberg, *The First Three Minutes: A Modern View of the Origin of the Universe* (New York: Bantam Books, 1979), p. 45.

11. Ibid., p. 68.

12. P. C. W. Davies, *Space and Time in the Modern Universe* (Cambridge: Cambridge University Press, 1977), pp. 167–168.

13. Steven Weinberg, *Three Minutes,* p. 4.

14. P. C. W. Davies, *Space and Time,* p. 159.

15. Ibid., p. 120.

16. Menachem M. Kasher, *Encyclopedia of Biblical Interpretation,* vol. I, trans. Harry Freedman (New York: American Biblical Encyclopedia Society, 1953), p. 5, citing Midrash in *Sefer Maaloth HaMidoth.*

17. *Hagigah* 15a (Talmud); Rashi's commentary on Gen. 1:2.

18. Steven Weinberg, *Three Minutes,* p. 45.

19. Ibid., p. 59.

20. Cf. Bob Toben, *Space, Time and Beyond: Toward an Explanation of the Unexplainable* (New York: Dutton, 1975), p. 47.

21. Stephen Toulmin, "The Charm of the Scout," in *New York Review of Books* (April 3, 1980): 38–41.

22. Ibid.

23. *Brain/Mind* Bulletin 4, no. 4 (Jan. 1, 1979): 3; cf. Harold J. Morowitz, "Rediscovering the Mind," in *Psychology Today* (August, 1980): 12 ff.

24. William Irwin Thompson, *Darkness and Scattered Light: Speculation on the Future* (New York: Doubleday, Anchor, 1978), p. 138.

25. Erich Neumann, *Origins and History,* p. 6.

26. Paul Davidovits, *Physics in Biology and Medicine* (Englewood Cliffs, N.J.: Prentice-Hall, 1975), p. 199; Arthur M. Young, *The Reflexive Universe: Evolution of Conciousness* (San Francisco: Delacorte Press, 1976), p. 12.

27. Ephraim F. Urbach, *The Sages: Their Concepts and Beliefs,* vol. II, trans. Israel Abrams (Jerusalem: Magnes Press, 1975), p. 781, note 21, quoting Philo Judaeus of Alexandria, *De Praemiis,* pp. 45–46.

28. Arthur M. Young, *The Reflexive Universe,* p. 11.

29. *Zohar* I 31b–32a.

30. Steven Weinberg, *Three Minutes,* pp. 69–79.

31. Gershom Scholem, *On the Kabbalah and Its Symbolism* (New York: Schocken, 1965), pp. 125–126.

32. *Pesikta de Rab Kahana, Kumi Uri* 21 (Midrash).

33. Lyall Watson, *Lifetide: The Biology of the Unconscious* (New York: Bantam Books, 1980), p. 73.

34. Cf. *Zohar* I 121b.

## CHAPTER 6: RETURNING TO NOTHING

1. Arthur Green, *Tormented Master: A Life of Rabbi Nahman of Bratslav* (University, Ala.: University of Alabama, 1979), pp. 344–345.
2. Paddy Chayevsky, *Altered States* (New York: Harper & Row, 1978), pp. 176–177.
3. Rabbi Dov Baer of Mezritch, *Maggid Devarav Leyakov,* ed. Rivka Schatz-Uffenheimer (Jerusalem: Magnes Press, 1976), p. 49, no. 30; cf. Martin Buber, *Tales of the Hasidim: The Early Masters,* trans. Olga Marx (New York: Schocken, 1947), p. 104.
4. *Pesachim* 116b (Talmud).
5. Arthur Waskow, *Godwrestling* (New York: Schocken, 1978), p. 93.
6. *Ketubot* 5a (Talmud).
7. Dov Baer, *Maggid,* p. 24, no. 9.
8. Cf. *Zohar* II 23a.
9. *Encyclopedia Judaica* (Jerusalem: Keter, 1971), vol. VII, p. 680, s.v. "Names of God."
10. Cf. Joseph Gikatilla, *Shaare Orah,* ed. Joseph Ben Shlomo (Jerusalem: Bialik Institute, 1970), p. 176.
11. *Exod. Rabba* 16.2 (Midrash); Nehama Leibowitz, *Studies in Shemot,* trans. Aryeh Newman (Jerusalem: World Zionist Organization, 1976), pp. 198–199.
12. Nahum N. Glatzer, ed., *The Passover Haggadah,* trans. Jacob Sloan (New York: Schocken, 1953), pp. 36–37; *Zohar* I 101b; *Talmud Jerushalmi, Sanhedrin* ch. 2, *Halakhah* 1, 7b (Talmud).
13. *Mekhilta de Rabbi Ishmael, D'Vayehi (Beshalah)* 5 (Midrash).
14. David de Sola Pool, ed. and trans., *Traditional Prayer Book for Sabbath and Festivals* (New York: Behrman House, 1960), pp. 7–8.
15. *Pirke de Rabbi Eliezer* 3 (Midrash).
16. Abraham Isaac Kook, *The Lights of Penitence,* trans. Ben Zion Bokser (New York: Paulist Press, 1978), p. 49.
17. Ibid., p. 56.
18. Lawrence Stone, *New York Review of Books* (Oct. 12, 1978): 22.
19. Joseph Campbell, *The Hero with a Thousand Faces,* 2d ed. (Princeton N.J.: Princeton University Press, 1949), p. 16.
20. Louis Jacobs, *Hasidic Prayer* (New York: Schocken, 1972), p. 78.
21. David de Sola Pool, *Traditional Prayer Book* (New York: Behrman House, 1960), pp. 7–8.
22. *Botzina Kadisha (Holy Light)* (Jerusalem, 1957), pp. 37–38.
23. Dov Baer, *Maggid,* p. 186, no. 110.

## CHAPTER 7: LIVING IN THE RIVER

1. Alan Watts, *This Is It* (New York: Random House, Vintage, 1973), p. 56.
2. Moses Maimonides, *The Guide for the Perplexed,* 2nd ed., trans. M. Friedlander (New York: Dover, 1956), p. 382.

3. Abraham Heschel, *The Earth Is the Lord's* bound with *The Sabbath* (New York: Harper & Row, Harper Torchbooks, 1966), "The Sabbath," p. 75.

4. Arthur Green, *Tormented Master: A Life of Rabbi Nahman of Bratslav* (University, Ala.: University of Alabama, 1979), p. 157, quoting *Likkutey MoHaran, Likket* 153.

5. Cf. Douglas R. Hofstadter, *Gödel Escher Bach: An Eternal Golden Braid* (New York: Basic Books, 1979).

6. Sigmund Freud, "Studies in Hysteria," in James Strachey, ed., *The Standard Edition of the Complete Works of Sigmund Freud* (London: Hogarth Press, 1953), p. 305.

# *Bring Spirituality into Your Daily Life*

## BEING GOD'S PARTNER
### How to Find the Hidden Link
### Between Spirituality and Your Work

by *Jeffrey K. Salkin*
Introduction by *Norman Lear*

A book that will challenge people of every denomination to reconcile the cares of work and soul. A groundbreaking book about spirituality and the work world, from a Jewish perspective. Helps the reader find God in the ethical striving and search for meaning in the professions and in business. Critiques our modern culture of workaholism and careerism, and offers practical suggestions for balancing your professional life and spiritual self.

**Being God's Partner** will inspire people of all faiths and no faith to find greater meaning in their work, and see themselves doing God's work in the world.

"His is an eloquent voice, bearing an important and concrete message of authentic Jewish religion. The book is engaging, easy to read and hard to put down — and it will make a difference and change people."
— Jacob Neusner, Distinguished Research Professor of Religious Studies, University of South Florida, author of *The Doubleday Anchor Reference Library Introduction to Rabbinic Literature*

6" x 9", 192 pp. Hardcover, ISBN 1-879045-37-0 **$19.95**

---

**NEW!**

## SELF, STRUGGLE & CHANGE
### Family Conflict Stories in Genesis
### and Their Healing Insights for Our Lives

by *Norman J. Cohen*

*How do I find greater wholeness in my life and in my family's life?*

The stress of late-20th-century living only brings new variations to timeless personal struggles. The people described by the biblical writers of Genesis were in situations and relationships very much like our own. We identify with them. Their stories still speak to us because they are about the same problems we deal with every day.

A modern master of biblical interpretation brings us greater understanding of the ancient text and of ourselves in this intriguing re-telling of conflict between husband and wife, father and son, brothers, and sisters.

"In this very human book, Rabbi Cohen renews our spirit, guiding us through our own struggle with faith as we confront the lives of each biblical character."
— Dr. Kerry Olitzky, author of *Sparks Beneath the Surface: A Spiritual Commentary on the Torah*

6" x 9", 224 pp. Hardcover, ISBN 1-879045-19-2 **$21.95**

---

## SEEKING THE PATH TO LIFE
### Theological Meditations On God
### and the Nature of People, Love, Life and Death

by *Rabbi Ira F. Stone,*
Ornamentation by *Annie Stone*

AWARD WINNER

For people who never thought they would read a book of theology—let alone understand it, enjoy it, savor it and have it affect the way they think about their lives.

In 45 intense meditations, each a page or two in length, Stone takes us on explorations of the most basic human struggles: life and death, love and anger, peace and war, covenant and exile.

"A bold book....The reader of any faith will be inspired, challenged and led more deeply into their own encounter with God."
— The Rev. Carla Berkedal, Episcopal Priest, Executive Director of Earth Ministry

6"x 9", 144 pp. Hardcover, ISBN 1-879045-17-6 **$19.95**

# *Spiritual Inspiration for Family Life*

## MOURNING & MITZVAH
### A Guided Journal for Walking the Mourner's Path Through Grief to Healing
by *Anne Brener, L.C.S.W.*  • WITH OVER 60 GUIDED EXERCISES •

*"Fully engaging in mourning means you will be a different person than before you began."*

For those who mourn a death, for those who would help them, for those who face a loss of any kind, Anne Brener teaches us the power and strength available to us in the fully experienced mourning process. Guided writing exercises help stimulate the processes of both conscious and unconscious healing.

"A stunning book! It offers an exploration in depth of the place where psychology and religious ritual intersect, and the name of that place is Truth."
> —Rabbi Harold Kushner, author of *When Bad Things Happen to Good People*

"This book is marvelous. It is a work that I wish I had written. It is the best book on this subject that I have ever seen." —Rabbi Levi Meier, Ph.D., Chaplain, Cedars Sinai Medical Center, Los Angeles, Orthodox Rabbi, Clinical Psychologist

7 1/2" x 9", 288 pp. Quality Paperback Original, ISBN 1-879045-23-0 **$19.95**

---

THE PREMIERE BOOK IN A
LANDMARK NEW 3-VOLUME SERIES

## *NEW!*

### LIFECYCLES
### Jewish Women on Life Passages & Personal Milestones

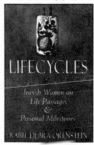

Edited and with introductions by *Rabbi Debra Orenstein*

In self-aware, passionate, and insightful voices, 50 leading thinkers come together to explore tradition and innovation in personal ritual and spirituality. Speaking to women of all backgrounds, it covers the entire spectrum of life's passages, from ceremonies around childbirth to new perspectives on aging. Other topics include marriage, singlehood, conversion, coming out, parenting, divorce, and midlife.

"An invaluable resource for women who want to connect Jewish feminism to the actual occasions of their lives. —Judith Plaskow, author of *Standing Again at Sinai: Judaism from a Feminist Perspective*

6" x 9", 480 pp. Hardcover, ISBN 1-879045-14-1 **$24.95**

---

## SO THAT YOUR VALUES LIVE ON
### Ethical Wills & How To Prepare Them
Edited by *Rabbi Jack Riemer & Professor Nathaniel Stampfer*

A cherished Jewish tradition, ethical wills—parents writing to children or grandparents to grandchildren—sum up what people have learned and express what they want most for, and from, their loved ones. Includes an intensive guide, "How to Write Your Own Ethical Will," and a topical index. A marvelous treasury of wills: Herzl, Sholom Aleichem, Israelis, Holocaust victims, contemporary American Jews.

"This remarkable volume will enrich all those who will read it and meditate upon its infinite widom."
— Elie Wiesel

6"x 9", 272 pp. Quality Paperback, ISBN 1-879045-34-6 **$16.95**  HC, ISBN -07-9 **$23.95**

# *Spiritual Inspiration for Family Life*

## NEW!

### IN GOD'S NAME

by *Sandy Eisenberg Sasso*
Full color illustrations by *Phoebe Stone*

**For children K-5**

Like an ancient myth in its poetic text and vibrant illustrations, this modern fable about the search for God's name celebrates the diversity and, at the same time, the unity of all the people of the world. Each seeker claims he or she alone knows the answer. Finally, they come together and learn what God's name really is, sharing the ultimate harmony of belief in one God by people of all faiths, all backgrounds.

"I got goosebumps when I read *In God's Name*, its language and illustrations are that moving. This is a book children will love and the whole family will cherish for its beauty and power."
—Francine Klagsbrun, author of *Mixed Feelings: Love, Hate, Rivalry, and Reconciliation among Brothers and Sisters*

9" x 12", 32 pp. Hardcover, Full color illus., ISBN 1-879045-26-5 **$16.95**

---

For Children
K-4

### GOD'S PAINTBRUSH

by *Sandy Eisenberg Sasso*
Full color illustrations by *Annette Compton*

MULTICULTURAL, NON-SECTARIAN, NON-DENOMINATIONAL. Invites children of all faiths and backgrounds to encounter God openly in their own lives. Wonderfully interactive, provides questions adult and child can explore together at the end of each episode.

"An excellent way to honor the imaginative breadth and depth of the spiritual life of the young." —Dr. Robert Coles, Harvard University

• AWARD WINNER •

11"x 8½", 32 pp. Hardcover, Full color illustrations, ISBN 1-879045-22-2 **$15.95**

---

### THE *NEW* JEWISH BABY BOOK
#### Names, Ceremonies, Customs — A Guide for Today's Families
by *Anita Diamant*
Foreword by *Rabbi Norman J. Cohen, Dean, HUC–JIR, NYC*
Introduction by *Rabbi Amy Eilberg*

A complete guide to the customs and rituals for welcoming a new child to the world and into the Jewish community, and for commemorating this joyous event in family life–whatever your family constellation. Updated, revised and expanded edition of the highly acclaimed *The Jewish Baby Book*. Includes new ceremonies for girls, celebrations in interfaith families. Also contains a unique directory of names that reflects the rich diversity of the Jewish experience.

"A book that all Jewish parents—no matter how religious—will find fascinating as well as useful. It is a perfect shower or new baby gift." — Pamela Abrams, Exec. Editor, *Parents Magazine*

6"x 9", 328 pp. Quality Paperback Original, ISBN 1-879045-28-1 **$15.95**

---

"Best
Religion Book
of the Year"

### PUTTING GOD ON THE GUEST LIST   AWARD WINNER
#### How to Reclaim the Spiritual Meaning
#### of Your Child's Bar or Bat Mitzvah
by *Rabbi Jeffrey K. Salkin*
Foreword by *Rabbi Sandy Eisenberg Sasso*
Introduction by *Rabbi William H. Lebeau, Vice Chancellor, JTS*

Joining explanation, instruction and inspiration, helps parent and child truly *be there* when the moment of Sinai is recreated in their lives. Asks and answers such fundamental questions as how did Bar and Bat Mitzvah originate? What is the lasting significance of the event? How to make the event more spiritually meaningful?

"Shows the way to restore spirituality and depth to every young Jew's most important rite of passage." — Rabbi Joseph Telushkin, author of *Jewish Literacy*

"I hope every family planning a Bar Mitzvah celebration reads Rabbi Salkin's book."
— Rabbi Harold S. Kushner, author of *When Bad Things Happen to Good People*

6"x 9", 184 pp. Quality Paperback, ISBN 1-879045-10-9 **$14.95** HC, ISBN -20-6 **$21.95**

# Add Greater Understanding to Your Life

# *Add Greater Meaning to Your Life*

# Motivation & Inspiration for Recovery

## TWELVE JEWISH STEPS TO RECOVERY
### A Personal Guide To Turning From Alcoholism & Other Addictions...Drugs, Food, Gambling, Sex

by *Dr. Kerry M. Olitzky* & *Stuart A. Copans, M.D.*
Preface by Abraham J. Twerski, M.D.
Introduction by Rabbi Sheldon Zimmerman
Illustrations by Maty Grünberg
"Getting Help" by JACS Foundation

A Jewish perspective on the Twelve Steps of addiction recovery programs with consolation, inspiration and motivation for recovery. It draws from traditional sources, and quotes from what recovering Jewish people say about their experiences with addictions of all kinds. Inspiring illustrations of the twelve gates of the Old City of Jerusalem.

6" x 9", 136 pp. Quality Paperback, ISBN 1-879045-09-5 **$12.95**   HC, ISBN -08-7 **$19.95**

---

## RENEWED EACH DAY
### Daily Twelve Step Recovery Meditations
### Based on the Bible
by *Dr. Kerry M. Olitzky* & *Aaron Z.*
**VOLUME I: Genesis & Exodus**
**VOLUME II: Leviticus, Numbers & Deuteronomy**

Using a seven day/weekly guide format, a recovering person and a spiritual leader who is reaching out to addicted people reflect on the traditional weekly Bible reading.

**Beautiful Two-Volume Slipcased Set**
6"x 9", V. I, 224 pp. / V. II, 280 pp., Quality Paperback Original, ISBN 1-879045-21-4 **$27.90**

---

## ONE HUNDRED BLESSINGS EVERY DAY
### Daily Twelve Step Recovery Affirmations,
### Exercises for Personal Growth & Renewal
### Reflecting Seasons of the Jewish Year
by *Dr. Kerry M. Olitzky*

4¹/2" x 6¹/2", Quality Paperback Original, 432 pp. ISBN 1-879045-30-3  **$14.95**

---

## RECOVERY FROM CODEPENDENCE
### A Jewish Twelve Steps Guide to Healing Your Soul

by *Dr. Kerry M. Olitzky*
Foreword by *Marc Galanter, M.D., Director,*
*Division of Alcoholism & Drug Abuse, NYU Medical Center*
Afterword by *Harriet Rossetto, Director, Gateways Beit T'shuvah*

For the estimated 90% of America struggling with the addiction of a family member or loved one, or involved in a dysfunctional family or relationship. A follow-up to the groundbreaking *Twelve Jewish Steps to Recovery.*

"The disease of chemical dependency is also a family illness. Rabbi Olitzky offers spiritual hope and support." —*Jerry Spicer, President, Hazelden*

"Another major step forward in finding the sources and resources of healing, both physical and spiritual, in our tradition." —*Rabbi Sheldon Zimmerman, Temple Emanu-El, Dallas, TX*

6" x 9", 160 pp. Quality Paperback Original, ISBN 1-879045-32-X **$13.95**   HC, ISBN -27-3 **$21.95**

# Order Information

| | |
|---|---|
| _____ | Aspects of Rabbinic Theology (pb), $18.95 |
| _____ | Being God's Partner (hc), $19.95 |
| _____ | The Empty Chair (hc), $ 9.95 |
| _____ | God's Paintbrush (hc), $15.95 |
| _____ | Healing of Soul, Healing of Body (pb), $13.95 |
| _____ | In God's Name (hc), $16.95 |
| _____ | The Last Trial (pb), $17.95 |
| _____ | Lifecycles, Volume One (hc), $24.95 |
| _____ | Mourning & Mitzvah (pb), $19.95 |
| _____ | The NEW Jewish Baby Book (pb), $15.95 |
| _____ | Putting God on the Guest List (hc), $21.95; (pb), $14.95 |
| _____ | Seeking the Path to Life (hc), $19.95 |
| _____ | Self, Struggle & Change (hc), $21.95 |
| _____ | So That Your Values Live On  (hc), $23.95; (pb), $16.95 |
| _____ | Spirit of Renewal (hc), $22.95; (pb), $16.95 |
| _____ | Tormented Master (pb), $17.95 |
| _____ | Your Word Is Fire (pb), $14.95 |

### • *The Kushner Series* •

The Book of Letters
 – Popular Hardcover Edition (hc), $24.95*
 – Deluxe Presentation Edition(hc), $79.95, *plus* $5.95 s/h
 – Collector's Limited Edition, $349.00, *plus* $12.95 s/h
The Book of Words (hc), $21.95*
God Was In This Place... (hc), $21.95; (pb) $16.95*
Honey from the Rock (pb), $14.95*
River of Light (pb), $14.95*
THE KUSHNER SERIES — 5 books *marked with asterisk above*, $93.75

### • *Motivation* & *Inspiration for Recovery* •

One Hundred Blessings Every Day, (pb) $14.95 *
Recovery From Codependence, (hc) $21.95;  (pb) $13.95*
Renewed Each Day, 2-Volume Set, (pb) $27.90*
Twelve Jewish Steps To Recovery, (hc) $19.95;  (pb) $12.95*

**THE COMPLETE RECOVERY SET – 20% SAVINGS**
**5 Books** *marked with asterisk above* + Print Portfolio — **$99.75**

*For s/h, add $3.00 for the first book, $1.50 each additional book*
All set prices include shipping/handling    **Total  $** _____

---

Check enclosed for $ _____ *payable to:* JEWISH LIGHTS Publishing

Charge my credit card:   ❏ MasterCard    ❏ Visa    ❏ Discover    ❏ AMEX

Credit Card # _____ Expires _____

Name on card _____

Signature _____ Phone ( _____ ) _____

Name _____

Street _____

City / State / Zip _____

---

*Phone, fax, or mail to:* JEWISH LIGHTS Publishing
Box 237, Sunset Farm Offices, Route 4, Woodstock, Vermont 05091
*Tel* (802) 457-4000    *Fax* (802) 457-4004
***Credit card orders*** (800) 962-4544 (9AM–5PM ET Monday–Friday)
*Generous discounts on quantity orders. SATISFACTION GUARANTEED. Prices subject to change.*
**AVAILABLE FROM BETTER BOOKSTORES.  TRY  YOUR BOOKSTORE FIRST.**